BRIDGE
The Complete Guide to Defensive Play

D0493543

BRIDGE BOOKS FROM ROBERT HALE

BRIDGE
The Complete
Guide to
Defensive Play

FRANK STEWART

Edited by
Derek Rimington

HALE
BRIDGE
BOOKS

ROBERT HALE · LONDON

© Frank Stewart 1988 and 1990
Originally published in the USA as
The Bridge Player's Comprehensive Guide to Defence
This revised edition first published in Great Britain 1990
First paperback edition 1994

ISBN 0 7090 5380 0

Robert Hale Limited
Clerkenwell House
Clerkenwell Green
London EC1R 0HT

Printed and bound by Interprint Ltd.,
Valletta, Malta.

Contents

Preface

Maybe you're an ambitious new bridge player who wants to learn all there is to know about good defensive technique; or perhaps you're an experienced player, but somehow you've let your considerable skills fall into decline. You may even be a true expert looking for one more mountain to climb. Whatever your station in the wonderful world of bridge, this book is for you.

Here are Quizzes on twenty-five of the most important areas of defensive play. Each one is introduced by example deals and an explanation of what the Quiz is all about. There are at least four problems in each Quiz. (This book contains over 160 problems, plus many illustrative full deals and single-suit diagrams, so the reader can look forward to as many hours of instruction and enjoyment as he or she can handle. As far as I know, *The Complete Guide to Defensive Play* is one of the most comprehensive quiz books on defensive play ever published. In fact, it is intended as a reference book as much as to entertain and test the reader.)

In most problems, the dealer and vulnerability are specified and the bidding is given. Unless otherwise indicated (as in Quiz 25, on defence at duplicate bridge), your goal is to *beat the contract* – don't worry about overtricks or extra undertricks. The solution for each problem includes the full deal.

You may assume that your opponents are competent – that they have bid correctly, and that declarer is handling the dummy capably. Unless otherwise noted, N-S are playing standard bidding methods. Nearly all INT openings show 16-18 HCP. Negative doubles make an occasional appearance. Other conventional bids are noted as they occur.

Don't feel badly if a lot of the answers elude you. While this admittedly is a book of Quizzes, and you may be looking forward to trying your skills, its real purpose is to provide instruction and improvement. As firm believers in the Socratic Method (so called because Socrates was antiquity's great teacher by question and answer), we think you will learn more if your thought processes are stimulated by questions. So whether you can provide the right answers or not, have fun and learn!

Quiz 1

The Crucial Trick: Opening Leads

If defence is the toughest part of bridge to master, as most writers maintain, then the opening lead must be the single most difficult aspect of the game. While it is possible to speculate on the best opening lead by listening carefully to the bidding and looking at one's own hand, there are woefully few times when an intelligently conceived opening lead will turn out to be a real 'killer'. The best anybody can aspire to is opening leads that are above average in the long run.

In considering his opening lead, a good defender always tries to imagine what declarer's plan will be. (See Quizzes 9, 10, and 13.) Often the bidding will clearly indicate what values declarer and dummy will have and how the play is likely to develop. The opening leader then launches his counter-measures while the defence enjoys the advantage of being on lead.

WEST	NORTH	EAST	SOUTH
		1 ♡	Pass
2 ♡	Pass	2 NT	Pass
3 ♡	All Pass		

South holds:
♠ J 10 9 6
♡ 8 5 3
♢ K 10 4
♣ A 9 3

Dummy will be very weak. The 2♡ response shows 6-9 HCP and, since West rejected partner's try for game, he should be in the lower end of that range. Also, South can expect dummy to be distributional rather than flat, since West expressed a clear preference for the suit contract. Therefore, dummy is likely to provide declarer with some ruffing tricks and little else – and a trump lead by South is automatic.

1

WEST	NORTH	EAST	SOUTH
		1 NT	Pass
2 NT	Pass	3 NT	All Pass

South holds:
♠ 10 6 5 4 2
♡ J 10
♢ 6 5 3
♣ Q 7 6

Staking the defence on the spades looks against the odds, since South lacks a ready entry. However, North is marked with a few points and probably has at least four hearts, since West made no effort to find a heart fit via Stayman. At IMPs or rubber bridge, many good players would try a heart lead. Even at matchpoints, a heart lead would have considerable support.

A little originality never hurts in choosing a good opening lead. E-W are vulnerable.

WEST	NORTH	EAST	SOUTH
		1 ♠	3 ♢
3 ♡	4 ♢	Pass	Pass
4 ♠	All Pass		

South holds:
♠ 6 5 4
♡ J 8 5 3
♢ K Q 10 9 6 2
♣ –

South should lead the ♢2. If partner is awake, he should grasp the suit-preference implications of this striking lead.

Suppose South's clubs and hearts were reversed. Now he should try leading the ♢Q. If partner wins the ace, he will see no future in leading another diamond. Perhaps he will find the right switch.

The value of opening lead problems is suspect because there aren't always any demonstrably clear-cut answers. Even a look at the deal that inspired the problem may prove little one way or another. In most cases I have refrained from cluttering up the page with a full deal, carefully constructed to prove that my suggested answer is correct. I could, of course, just as easily construct a deal that would make my recommendation a disaster. This quiz is intended to illustrate some of the lines of reasoning that guide a good player in choosing consistently effective opening leads.

Problems
(Throughout, neither side is vulnerable.)

1.

WEST	NORTH	EAST	SOUTH
		1 ♡	Pass
2 ♢	Pass	2 ♡	Pass
4 ♡	All Pass		

South holds:
♠ K 10 3
♡ 9 6 3
♢ A 3
♣ 10 9 8 6 3

2.

WEST	NORTH	EAST	SOUTH
		1 ♠	Pass
2 ♡	Pass	2 ♠	Pass
3 ♣	Pass	4 ♠	All Pass

South holds:
♠ 5
♡ K J 9 5 3
♢ K 10 5
♣ J 10 8 3

3.

WEST	NORTH	EAST	SOUTH
		1 ♡	Pass
2 ♡	All Pass		

South holds:
♠ 10 9 5
♡ 7 6 5 2
♢ K 9 5 3
♣ A J

4.

WEST	NORTH	EAST	SOUTH
		1 ◇	All Pass

South holds:
✓ ♠ J 10 3
♡ A J 7 5 2 ✗
◇ 4 3
♣ J 7 6

5.

WEST	NORTH	EAST	SOUTH
		1 ♡	Pass
2 ♣	Pass	4 ♣	Pass
4 ♡	All Pass		

South holds:
✓ ♠ Q J 10 8 3
♡ 4 3
◇ J 3
♣ A 8 7 5

Solutions

1. ♠3. The defence must establish tricks quickly, before declarer can draw trumps and set up dummy's diamonds. The most aggressive lead available is recommended. This is not the time to lead your ace 'to look at dummy'.

2. ♣J. This time your length and strength in hearts will prevent declarer from setting up dummy's suit, so a passive lead is in order.

3. ♡2. Dummy will be weakish, so there is no hurry to seek out tricks. This lead also might deprive declarer of a ruff in dummy. The lead of the ♣A is against the odds, especially since the power of your jack might be wasted. Because you have four trumps, you aren't sure you want to ruff anyway.

4. Diamond. Partner must have good diamonds, or else he would have protected. Perhaps your best move is to try to draw trumps.

5. ♣A, planning to continue the suit. Your partner is an odds-on favourite to have a club singleton or void.

Problems

6.

WEST	NORTH	EAST	SOUTH
		1 NT	Pass
4 NT	Pass	6 NT	All Pass

South holds:
♠ Q 10 7 6 3
♡ A 10 4
♢ J 10 9
♣ 9 2

7.

WEST	NORTH	EAST	SOUTH
		1 ♡	Pass
2 ♠	Pass	3 ♡	Pass
3 ♣	Pass	3 NT	Pass
4 ♡	Pass	5 ♡	Pass
6 ♡	All Pass		

South holds:
♠ A 3
♡ 7 6 4
♢ K 4 3
♣ 10 9 7 5 3

8.

WEST	NORTH	EAST	SOUTH
		1 ♡	Pass
3 ♣	Pass	3 NT	Pass
6 NT	All Pass		

South holds:
♠ K J 6 2
♡ J 9 6 4
♢ 7 6 5
♣ 9 2

9.

WEST	NORTH	EAST	SOUTH
		1 ♠	Pass
2 NT¹	Pass	3 ♠	Pass
4 ♠	All Pass		

¹ forcing

South holds:
♠ Q 9 3
♡ J 10 8 3
♢ A 10 6
♣ K J 7

10.

WEST	NORTH	EAST	SOUTH
		1 ♡	Pass
2 ♣	Pass	3 ♡	Pass
4 ♡	All Pass		

South holds:
♠ K Q 10 7
♡ K 8 5 3
♢ 7
♣ A 9 5 2

Solutions

6. ♢10. Partner has no high cards, so leading away from the ♠Q could be costly. Nor should you bang down the ♡A and set up declarer's honours. Stay passive, and perhaps you will score two tricks in the majors. The deceptive lead of the *ten* is unlikely to cost your side anything – you can afford to deceive partner when he'll play no part in the defence. Against 3 NT, you would, of course, lead a spade.

7. ♢3. With dummy's spades an obvious threat, declarer has the material to take twelve tricks in due time. You must try to establish a second trick.

8. ♠2. This is not the time to go passive, with both East and West holding long suits. Compare with Problem 6.

9. ♡J. A normal, passive lead is preferred, since dummy will have a balanced hand with few discards for declarer's losers.

10. ♠K. Your hand is too strong to lead the singleton diamond – partner will never get in to give you a ruff. Also, you have four trumps, so a forcing defence might work better than trying for ruffs.

Problems

11.

WEST	NORTH	EAST	SOUTH
		1 ♣	Pass
1 ♠	Pass	1 NT	Pass
3 NT	All Pass		

South holds:
♠ 7 6 4
♡ A 6 5
♢ K 4
♣ Q J 10 3 2

12.

WEST	NORTH	EAST	SOUTH
	1 ♢	1 ♠	Pass
2 ♢¹	Dbl	Pass	Pass
3 ♠	Pass	4 ♠	All Pass

¹ good hand, spade support

South holds:
♠ 7 6 4
♡ J 10 3
♢ Q 10 5 4
♣ J 10 4

13.

WEST	NORTH	EAST	SOUTH
1 ♢	Pass	1 ♠	Pass
2 ♡	Pass	2 NT	Pass
3 ♠	Pass	3 NT	All Pass

South holds:
♠ A Q 4
♡ 5 4
♢ K J 9 8 4
♣ J 9 3

14.

WEST	NORTH	EAST	SOUTH
	1 ♡	1 ♠	Pass
1 NT	Pass	2 ♠	Pass
3 ♠	All Pass		

South holds:
♠ 9 6 5 3
♡ Q 9 5
◇ J 2
♣ 10 7 5 3

15.

WEST	NORTH	EAST	SOUTH
		1 ♡	Pass
1 ♠	Pass	1 NT	Pass
2 NT	All Pass		

South holds:
♠ 9 3
♡ Q 10 8 3
◇ Q 9 4 2
♣ A 9 3

Solutions

11.   ♣3. Despite declarer's bid, the club suit offers your best hope to beat the contract. Leading *low* despite your sequence is best when declarer is known to have club length. This gains when partner has a doubleton ace, king or nine.

On other occasions, you might avoid the normal fourth-best lead from a long, broken suit and try your lowest instead. If declarer has bid the suit, your fourth-highest card might be too valuable to waste.

12.   ◇Q. This may be the only time you'll ever be on lead. The lead of the queen may allow you to hold the lead and make a good switch through dummy:

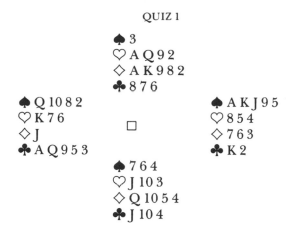

♠ 3
♡ A Q 9 2
◇ A K 9 8 2
♣ 8 7 6

♠ Q 10 8 2
♡ K 7 6
◇ J
♣ A Q 9 5 3

♠ A K J 9 5
♡ 8 5 4
◇ 7 6 3
♣ K 2

♠ 7 6 4
♡ J 10 3
◇ Q 10 5 4
♣ J 10 4

13. ◇J. 'Surrounding plays' can be made on the opening lead. If the diamond situation is

$$5\ 3$$

A Q 7 2   □   10 6

K J 9 8 4

you must not start your fourth-best card. Incidentally, leading the unbid suit would be most unwise. Declarer is bound to have good clubs on this auction; since he lacks a good fit for the red suits, he may have as many as five clubs. Put your faith in diamonds, despite the opening bid.

14. ♡Q. A forcing defence is your best chance. With dummy marked with something in hearts and declarer likely to be short, the honour lead is most likely to accomplish something. The hearts, for instance, may lie this way:

$$A\ J\ 8\ 6\ 3$$

K 7 4 2   □   10

Q 9 5

15. ♠9. The opponents have limited values, and declarer may find it hard to assemble eight tricks without help. Neither the hearts, where you have a double stopper, nor spades, where partner should have some length, is likely to be productive. There is no reason to lead a diamond (and possibly give away a vital trick) when the contract may die of natural causes *whether or not you establish a suit.*

Problems

16.

WEST	NORTH	EAST	SOUTH
		Pass	Pass
1 ♡	Pass	1 NT	Pass
Pass	Dbl	All Pass	

South holds:
♠ Q 10 7 5 2
♡ J 3
◇ A 7 6
♣ Q 10 7

17.

WEST	NORTH	EAST	SOUTH
			1 NT
Pass	2 ♣	Pass	2 ◇
Pass	Pass	2 ♡	All Pass

South holds:
♠ A J 3
♡ K 7 6
◇ A 10 4
♣ A 7 6 5

18.

WEST	NORTH	EAST	SOUTH
		3 NT[1]	All Pass

[1] 'Gambling', with a long , running minor and no outside ace or king.

South holds:
♠ A 7 5
♡ Q 6
◇ 7 6 3
♣ K J 9 5 3

19.

WEST	NORTH	EAST	SOUTH
	1 ♣	Pass	Pass
1 ♡	Pass	1 NT	Pass
2 NT	Pass	3 NT	Pass
Pass	Dbl	All Pass	

South holds:
- ♠ 10 8 3
- ♡ Q 7 4
- ♢ 10 8 6 4 2
- ♣ 9 3

20.

WEST	NORTH	EAST	SOUTH
		1 ♢	1 ♠
2 ♢	Pass	2 NT	Pass
3 NT	Dbl	All Pass	

South holds:
- ♠ K J 9 7 5
- ♡ Q 10 6 5
- ♢ A 5
- ♣ J 2

21.

WEST	NORTH	EAST	SOUTH
		1 ♢	Pass
1 ♠	Pass	2 ♢	Pass
3 ♢	Pass	3 NT	Pass
Pass	Dbl	All Pass	

South holds:
- ♠ J 5
- ♡ Q 10 8 5 2
- ♢ J 9 3
- ♣ 8 7 2

22.

WEST	NORTH	EAST	SOUTH
		1 NT	Pass
3 NT	Dbl	All Pass	

South holds:
- ♠ K 10 8 6 3
- ♡ 9
- ♢ J 9 6 5
- ♣ 8 6 5

Solutions

16.♡J. Partner has a good hand with heart length and strength.

17. ♣A, intending to lead another club. Partner planned to pass any response to his Stayman inquiry, so he has a weak hand with length in diamonds, spades and hearts.

18. The standard lead against this bidding is the ♠A. East should have seven solid diamonds, so your best chance to beat 3 NT is to run one of the black suits. You will switch to clubs or hearts if partner discourages a spade continuation.

19. ♣9. Partner's double conventionally demands the lead of his suit.

20. ♠7. Partner's double asks you to lead your own suit. He has help in your suit and wants to make sure you lead it.

21. ♠J. Partner's double conventionally requests the lead of dummy's first-bid suit.

22. ♡9. After this unrevealing bidding, partner's double conventionally requires you to make an *unusual* lead. Usually this will be your shortest suit (unless, perhaps, you have an honour there).

Problems

23.

WEST	NORTH	EAST	SOUTH
1♢	1♠	2♡	Pass
4♡	Pass	5♣	Pass
6♡	Dbl	All Pass	

South holds:
♠9 7 5 3
♡8
♢Q 9 7 5 2
♣J 7 3

24.

WEST	NORTH	EAST	SOUTH
		1 ♠	Pass
2 ♣	Pass	2 ◇	Pass
3 ◇	Pass	4 ◇	Pass
5 ◇	All Pass		

South holds:
♠ Q 6 4
♡ A Q 9 3
◇ 10 6 4
♣ 9 7 3

25.

WEST	NORTH	EAST	SOUTH
		1 NT	Pass
3 NT	All Pass		

South holds:
♠ J 8 7
♡ Q 10 6 2
◇ Q 10 6 2
♣ A 2

26.

WEST	NORTH	EAST	SOUTH
		1 ♠	Pass
3 ♠	Pass	4 NT	Pass
5 ♡	Pass	5 NT	Pass
6 ♣	Pass	6 ♠	All Pass

South holds:
♠ Q 8 4
♡ J 9 7 5 3
◇ Q 6 5
♣ 10 3

27.

WEST	NORTH	EAST	SOUTH
1 ♣	Pass	1 NT	Pass
2 NT	Pass	3 NT	All Pass

South holds:
♠ A Q 10 6 2
♡ 8 7
◇ K 8 5 3
♣ 9 4

Solutions

23. ◇5. Partner's 'Lightner' double of this voluntarily bid slam bars you from leading his suit. Normally, the lead of dummy's first-bid suit is suggested, since this is a lead you would seldom consider without partner's double.

24. ♡A. A trump lead is out when both dummy and declarer have bid side suits; your heart tricks might disappear unless you take them immediately. The opponents avoided 3 NT, so perhaps partner has the ♡K.

25. ♡2. Prefer the major suit to the minor, since West failed to investigate a major-suit contract.

26. ◇5. You are entitled to draw a negative inference from partner's failure to double either of West's responses to Blackwood.

```
                      ♠ 7
                      ♡ 10 4 2
                      ◇ K 9 8 4 2
                      ♣ 8 6 5 2
  ♠ A 10 6 3                       ♠ K J 9 5 2
  ♡ A Q 8                          ♡ K 6
  ◇ J 3              □             ◇ A 10 7
  ♣ Q J 7 4                        ♣ A K 9
                      ♠ Q 8 4
                      ♡ J 9 7 5 3
                      ◇ Q 6 5
                      ♣ 10 3
```

Such clues also are available when partner fails to double a control-showing cue-bid or a bid of the fourth suit, which is often made with a fragment or single stopper.

27. ♠Q. Another 'surrounding' theme. If dummy holds K-J-x of spades, your cause is hopeless; but if the situation is

```
              8 7
     K 9 4     □     J 5 3
           A Q 10 6 2
```

the queen might strike an advantage. The queen would be clearly right if you had no side cards, while the lead of the ace would be attractive if you had more than one possible entry.

Quiz 2

Second-Hand Play

The well-known admonition to play 'second hand low' is a throwback to the time of whist and auction bridge. While 'second hand low' is still a fairly reliable guide for routine situations, it should be regarded as a tendency, not as a hard and fast rule.

The reason for playing low as second hand is simple: Partner is last to play, so there is less reason for second hand to do anything desperate. Second hand can *wait* and let declarer commit himself, often to his disadvantage, as third hand. If you play low as second hand, you might oblige declarer to guess what to play from third hand, force him to spend a high card to keep fourth hand from winning cheaply, avoid clashing with one of your partner's high cards on the same trick, or make declarer's job of establishing winners a little harder.

In this situation:

```
               N.
              8 7 4            E
   J 9 5         □          A 10 6 3
              K Q 2
               S
```

declarer may be entitled to two tricks, but if East plays low the first time the suit is led from dummy, declarer must spend an entry to lead the suit again. And if declarer's holding were K-J-2, he would have to guess whether to play the king or the jack after second hand's duck.

```
               J 6
  A Q 8 3        □            9 4
             K 10 7 5 2
```

Needing to establish some tricks here, declarer leads low toward the jack. West can save a trick in the long run by ducking.

15

A J 8
K Q 6   ☐   9 4 3
10 7 5 2

When declarer leads low toward dummy, West does best to play low, forcing declarer to guess. Declarer's percentage play is a finesse of dummy's eight, winning when West has the nine plus either the king or queen. West would 'split his honours,' as we say, only if he wanted just one fast trick.

The most spectacular example of second-hand ducking I can remember occurred in an international event when Italy's Benito Garozzo defended a spade part-score contract with A-K-x-x of hearts in front of dummy's Q-10-8-x. Garozzo refrained from leading a heart, choosing a trump lead instead. At one point, declarer led a heart toward dummy. Garozzo played low, and declarer tried dummy's eight, losing to the nine. Later on, declarer got back in and led another low heart towards dummy. Garozzo played low again (!), and this time the ten lost to the jack.

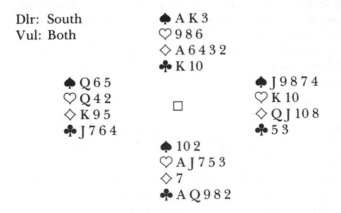

Dlr: South   ♠ A K 3
Vul: Both   ♡ 9 8 6
             ◇ A 6 4 3 2
             ♣ K 10

♠ Q 6 5   ♠ J 9 8 7 4
♡ Q 4 2   ☐   ♡ K 10
◇ K 9 5   ◇ Q J 10 8
♣ J 7 6 4   ♣ 5 3

            ♠ 10 2
            ♡ A J 7 5 3
            ◇ 7
            ♣ A Q 9 8 2

On this deal from the 1983 Bermuda Bowl semifinals, two N-S pairs stopped at a heart game while the other two reached the shaky slam. Declarer won the spade lead and played a trump. If East follows with the ten, declarer inserts the jack, wins the return, and cashes the ♡A, dropping the king. Now a third round of clubs can be ruffed, and South re-enters his hand with a diamond ruff to draw West's last trump.

In the Bermuda Bowl, however, *all four* Easts (Peter Weichsel and Eddie Wold of the United States, Michel Lebel of France, and Soldano De Falco of Italy) put up the ♡K. Two declarers then went to the ♣K to lead a second heart – ten, jack, queen. West played a third trump and scored a trick with the ♣J. The other two declarers immediately switched to clubs, but East overruffed dummy on the third round, and West still had to make his trump queen.

A situation players find vexing occurs when declarer leads a low card toward dummy's K-Q-x-x and you just know it's a singleton – the urge to grab your ace may be overpowering.

```
                    ♠ K Q 5 3
                    ♡ J 9 6 4
                    ◇ 7 5
                    ♣ J 6 4
    ♠ A 10 7 2                        ♠ J 9 6 4
    ♡ K 5                             ♡ 2
    ◇ Q 10 8 4          □            ◇ A 9 3 2
    ♣ K 9 3                          ♣ Q 10 7 5
                    ♠ 8
                    ♡ A Q 10 8 7 3
                    ◇ K J 6
                    ♣ A 8 2
```

WEST	NORTH	EAST	SOUTH
			1 ♡
Dbl	2 ♡	2 ♠	4 ♡
All Pass			

You, West, decide to lead the ◇4 against the 4♡ contract. Partner wins the ace and returns the two to declarer's king. Now comes the inevitable low spade from declarer. What do you do?

No doubt partner should have found the club switch, but you must deal with things as they are. You know that declarer has three diamonds (from partner's return of the two), one spade, and probably six hearts (to justify his jump to game – he has at most only sixteen points in high cards). If declarer has both ♣A and ♣Q, you aren't going to beat this. But partner might have the ♣Q, especially since he declined to switch to clubs. In that case you can beat it *if you duck this trick*. Declarer will lose no spades, but he'll have two club losers. Note the outcome if you rise with the ♠A

Another way of looking at it is counting declarer's tricks. He has five hearts, a diamond, a diamond ruff, and the ♣A, so unless he has the ♣Q as well, one spade trick won't be enough.

Positions like this are common. In general, you should *win* when you have defensive tricks ready to cash or when there is no sign of any defensive tricks except your ace. You should *duck* when the contract is in doubt, there are possible defensive tricks on the horizon and declarer will gain on the transaction if you win.

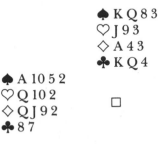

        ♠ K Q 8 3
        ♡ J 9 3
        ◇ A 4 3
        ♣ K Q 4

♠ A 10 5 2
♡ Q 10 2   □
◇ Q J 9 2
♣ 8 7

Dummy opened 1 NT; declarer responded 3♡ and was raised to 4♡. You, West, lead the ◇Q. Dummy wins and partner plays the eight, encouraging. Declarer cashes the ♡AK, partner showing out on the second round, and leads a spade. Rise, cash whatever diamond tricks you can, and retire. Declarer has the ♣A, so the issue is in no doubt.

There are several other times when it is proper to break the second hand low tendency:

- You often want to play high from a sequence of cards, to let partner know about your holding.
- Many deceptive plays are associated with second hand high. See Quiz 23.
- Sometimes you can take a trick or prevent declarer from winning a trick too cheaply if you play high, and *it costs you nothing* to do so. In particular, many cash-out situations require you to grab a winner in second seat.

This deal arose in the 1973 Bermuda Bowl. South, believe it or not, was a many-time world champion.

Dlr: South
Vul: N-S

```
                    ♠ Q 5
                    ♡ A K 9 4
                    ◇ J
                    ♣ K 9 8 7 6 5
    ♠ 10 8 4 2                      ♠ A J 9 7 6 3
    ♡ 8 7                           ♡ Q 10 6 5
    ◇ 10 8 3 2         □           ◇ A Q 7
    ♣ Q 10 3                        ♣ –
                    ♠ K
                    ♡ J 3 2
                    ◇ K 9 6 5 4
                    ♣ A J 4 2
```

WEST	NORTH	EAST	SOUTH
			1 ◇
Pass	1 ♡	1 ♠	2 ♡
2 ♠	3 ♣	4 ♠	Pass
Pass	Dbl	All Pass	

In N-S's style, the 3♣ bid showed at least a five-card suit and a
good hand. South led a heart to the king, and North shifted to
the ◇J. Declarer went up with the ◇A, cashed the ♠A, and led
the ◇7 away from the queen.

At this point, South had an aberration, playing low. North
ruffed dummy's ◇10 and cashed the ♡A, but declarer took the
rest, throwing two diamonds from dummy on the ♡Q and ♡10.

The following deal, entitled 'second hand middle,' was
reported by Eddie Kantar in 1978 and won a Bols Brilliancy
Prize for Eddie's partner, Billy Eisenberg, who sat West.

Dlr: South
Vul: Both

```
                    ♠ A 9
                    ♡ Q 9 8 4 2
                    ◇ J 10 6 3
                    ♣ K 8
    ♠ K J 6 5                        ♠ 10 7 4
    ♡ A J 5                          ♡ 10 7 6
    ◇ 9 5 2           □             ◇ K 7 4
    ♣ 10 9 6                         ♣ Q J 5 4
                    ♠ Q 8 3 2
                    ♡ K 3
                    ◇ A Q 8
                    ♣ A 7 3 2
```

WEST	NORTH	EAST	SOUTH
			1 NT
Pass	2 ♣	Pass	2 ♠
Pass	3 ♡	Pass	3 NT
All Pass			

Eisenberg led the ♣10 – king, five, two. A diamond to the queen won, and declarer continued with the ♡3. Here, Eisenberg put up his *jack*, and the queen won in dummy. Two more rounds of diamonds picked up the suit, and declarer exited with the ♡K to West's ace. Eisenberg now led the ♣9, ducked all around, and another club to declarer's ace. Declarer played to the ♠A and cashed the thirteenth diamond, but he could make no more tricks. *East* won the next heart, cashed the good club, and led a spade. Down one.

Had West followed low to the first heart, he would have been end-played on the third round of hearts and forced to concede the ninth trick to the ♠Q. (Kantar pointed out that it would do West no good to discard the ♡J on the fourth diamond – declarer could play ♠A and ♠9, covering with the queen if East played the ten. The ♠8 would have to score.)

Our Quiz may call upon you to avoid playing second hand low in several other situations.

Problems

1. **Dlr: North**   ♠ A J 8 3
    Vul: N-S   ♡ 7 6 3
                        ◇ A K J 9 2
                        ♣ 5

                                    ♠ 6 5 2
                        □   ♡ K J 8
                                    ◇ 8 7 6 5
                                    ♣ A 10 3

WEST	NORTH	EAST	SOUTH
	1 ◇	Pass	1 ♠
Pass	3 ♠	Pass	4 NT
Pass	5 ♡	Dbl	6 ♠
All Pass			

West, your partner, leads the ♡4, and your jack forces declarer's ace. Declarer draws trumps in three rounds, West following twice. Now South produces the ◇Q and runs five diamond tricks, throwing one heart and two clubs. You let go a heart. At trick ten, the ♣5 is led from dummy. Your play? Quickly!

2. Dlr: West   ♠ A J 9
   Vu: None   ♡ A 6 5
                  ◇ J 5 3
                  ♣ A K 9 8

   ♠ Q 10 4
   ♡ K Q J 8 2   □
   ◇ A
   ♣ Q 7 5 4

WEST	NORTH	EAST	SOUTH
1 ♡	1 NT	Pass	3 ◇
Pass	3 ♡	Pass	5 ◇
All Pass			

You, West, lead the ♡K to dummy's ace. Declarer ruffs a heart and plays the ◇K. You win the ace and exit with a heart, ruffed. Declarer cashes the ♣A, discards a spade on the ♣K, ruffs a club, returns to the ◇J, and ruffs dummy's last club. Now a spade is led. What do you play and why?

Solutions

1. You must *duck* as smoothly as possible. Count declarer's tricks: He has four spades, five diamonds, one heart, and one ruff for a total of eleven, so he can't make it without one club trick. If he has both the ♣K and ♣Q or just the king, there is nothing you can do; but if South has the ♣K and ♣J, you have a chance so long as you put him to a guess on this trick.

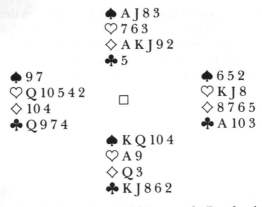

♠ A J 8 3
♥ 7 6 3
♦ A K J 9 2
♣ 5

♠ 9 7
♥ Q 10 5 4 2
♦ 10 4
♣ Q 9 7 4

♠ 6 5 2
♥ K J 8
♦ 8 7 6 5
♣ A 10 3

♠ K Q 10 4
♥ A 9
♦ Q 3
♣ K J 8 6 2

2. The deal is from the 1966 Bermuda Bowl, with the late Lew Mathe sitting West. The end position was:

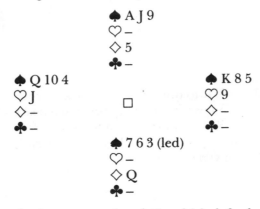

♠ A J 9
♥ –
♦ 5
♣ –

♠ Q 10 4
♥ J
♦ –
♣ –

♠ K 8 5
♥ 9
♦ –
♣ –

♠ 7 6 3 (led)
♥ –
♦ Q
♣ –

Mathe alertly put up the ♠Q, which left declarer with no chance.

The full deal:

♠ A J 9
♥ A 6 5
♦ J 5 3
♣ A K 9 8

♠ Q 10 4
♥ K Q J 8 2
♦ A
♣ Q 7 5 4

♠ K 8 5
♥ 9 7 4 3
♦ 8 4
♣ J 10 3 2

♠ 7 6 3 2
♥ 10
♦ K Q 10 9 7 6 2
♣ 6

Had Mathe played low, declarer would have inserted dummy's nine, end-playing East.

Declarer could, and should, have made the contract by playing on spades earlier, but even the best can err. South was the great Italian Pietro Forquet.

Problems

3. Dlr: West   ♠ 8 7 4
    Vul: N-S   ♡ Q 6 4 3
                  ♢ Q 7 5 3
                  ♣ A 9

    ♠ A Q 9 3
    ♡ K 10 8   □
    ♢ 8
    ♣ J 10 8 4 2

WEST	NORTH	EAST	SOUTH
Pass	Pass	Pass	1 ♢
Dbl	2 ♢	2 ♠	5 ♢
All Pass			

You, West, lead the ♣J. Dummy's ace wins, East signalling with the seven. Declarer ruffs a club, draws a round of trumps, to which your partner follows with the ten, and leads out the ♡A. How do you defend?

4. Dlr: South   ♠ 6 4 2
    Vul: Both   ♡ A K Q 9 4
                  ♢ 6 5
                  ♣ 7 3 2

    ♠ 9 5 3
    ♡ J 2   □
    ♢ K J 9 4 2
    ♣ Q 10 4

WEST	NORTH	EAST	SOUTH
			1 ♣
Pass	1 ♡	Pass	2 NT
Pass	3 ♡	Pass	3 NT
All Pass			

You, West, lead the ♢4. Declarer, who has A-10-x, holds off the ace until the third round. At trick four, declarer leads a low heart towards dummy. What do you play and why?

Solutions

3.   You should drop the ♡K under the ace. Declarer appears to have seven diamonds, a club, and no more than two spades, so he has at least three hearts. East can be expected to hold the ♡J, else declarer would have taken a finesse in the suit. You must hope that the full deal is:

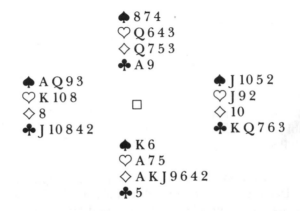

♠ 8 7 4
♡ Q 6 4 3
♢ Q 7 5 3
♣ A 9

♠ A Q 9 3
♡ K 10 8
♢ 8
♣ J 10 8 4 2

♠ J 10 5 2
♡ J 9 2
♢ 10
♣ K Q 7 6 3

♠ K 6
♡ A 7 5
♢ A K J 9 6 4 2
♣ 5

If you hold on to the ♡K, declarer can set up dummy's fourth heart without letting your partner in to play a spade through the king. (South is marked with the ♠K. He could hardly have enough to bid an eleven-trick game, vulnerable against not, without it.)

Note that if declarer had led a low heart first, the right defence would be no less easy. You would have to play your *ten*, letting dummy's queen win, and then jettison your king if declarer led to the ace.

4.   Play the ♡J. If you do not, declarer, who is likely to have two low hearts on the bidding, will insert dummy's nine, passing his heart loser to your partner, who has no more diamonds. Declarer will win any return and take three spades, four hearts, a club and a diamond. The full deal:

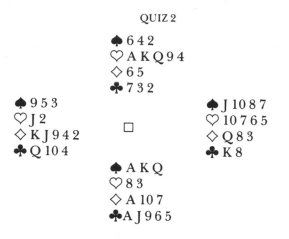

♠ 6 4 2
♡ A K Q 9 4
◇ 6 5
♣ 7 3 2

♠ 9 5 3
♡ J 2
◇ K J 9 4 2
♣ Q 10 4

♠ J 10 8 7
♡ 10 7 6 5
◇ Q 8 3
♣ K 8

♠ A K Q
♡ 8 3
◇ A 10 7
♣ A J 9 6 5

Even if you defend correctly, partner must make a good second-hand play to defeat the contract. Declarer must win the first heart, of course, lest you cash your diamonds, and now he is limited to just three heart tricks. However, if declarer now leads a club, partner must play his ♣K. If partner follows with the ♣8, declarer can cash his spades and exit with a club, forcing a heart lead into dummy's tenace.

Quiz 3

Should You Cover?

A further exception to the 'second hand low' tendency arises when declarer *leads a high card*. In that case, a defender might gain by covering with a high card of his own. The idea is that if declarer is obliged to spend two of his high cards on the same trick, some of the defenders' lower-ranking cards may be promoted quickly to winning status.

Q 5
   □
9 8 4 3   K 7 2
A J 10 6

If declarer leads the queen from dummy, East can gain a trick by covering with the king.

There are many lesser-known positions. For example:

10 4
   □
Q 9 6 3   A 5
K J 8 7 2

If declarer leads the ten, East can gain a trick by 'covering' with the ace.

In these first two instances note that declarer led an *unsupported* high card. But if this is the position:

J 10 9 8
□
       Q 7 6 3

East should duck if the jack is led, since the defenders clearly have no intermediate cards to promote.

In the in-between cases, where declarer's holding is headed by a couple of honours but isn't completely solid, it is generally correct to cover the *second* honour.

```
                        J 10 4
      K 9 5 3             □              Q 8 2
                        A 7 6
```

East should duck if the jack is led, but should cover the ten if it is led later. Declarer will be held to just one trick. However:

```
                        10 9 4
      K 8 7 2             □              A J 3
                        Q 6 5
```

If dummy leads the ten, East, with *two* honours of his own, must cover to keep declarer from winning a trick. And:

```
                        J 10 8
      K 5 4              □              Q 9
                        A 7 6 3 2
```

This time East must cover the first honour to give the defence a chance for two tricks. That's what makes bridge such a difficult game – there are exceptions to the exceptions to the rules!

The following deal was presented by Bobby Wolff in 'The Aces on Bridge', his syndicated column.

```
Dlr: South          ♠ J 8 4
Vul: Both           ♡ A 7
                    ◇ K 9 8 7 6 5
                    ♣ J 2
      ♠ 6 3                          ♠ Q 10 9 5 2
      ♡ Q J 10 8 4                   ♡ 6 5 2
      ◇ Q 10 4 2        □            ◇ 3
      ♣ K 7                          ♣ A 8 6 4
                    ♠ A K 7
                    ♡ K 9 3
                    ◇ A J
                    ♣ Q 10 9 5 3
```

South plays in 3 NT, and West leads the ♡Q. Declarer wins with the king and plays the ◇A and ◇J. Should West cover?

Clearly, the answer is no. True, West can promote one trick for his ten by covering. But if West plays low, declarer cannot establish and cash dummy's diamonds.

The position below is somewhat enigmatic.

Q J 4 3
□   K 2

Should East cover the lead of the jack or queen? Not to cover will be disastrous if declarer has A-7-6-5. However, if declarer holds A-9-8-7 (which is more likely), he will look with favour on a cover – he can win and pass the nine next, bringing in the suit. But if East ducks smoothly on the first round, declarer must guess whether to continue with dummy's other honour or a low card. (West, for his part, can lead declarer astray by dropping his middle spot from 10-x-x on the first round.)

Clearly, the defenders have it easier if *dummy* is the hand leading to the trick. If *declarer* leads, his holding is concealed and some unpleasant guessing may be required. Would you cover an honour in this situation?

Dlr: South   ♠ A 6 3
Vul: None   ♡ 7 6 3
               ◇ A 10 4
               ♣ J 9 6 3

♠ 10 8 4
♡ K 10 8 4 2
◇ Q 5 2   □
♣ K 4

South opened 1 NT and was raised to 3 NT. Your heart lead is covered by the three, jack and queen. Now South leads the ◇J.

It would be right to cover if declarer's holding was J-x or J-x-x, but if he had that, he'd be unlikely to attack diamonds at an early stage. Probably, diamonds are declarer's best suit – he might have K-J-9-8-(x). He is tempting you to cover to solve his problems. An experienced player anticipates a problem like this from the moment he sees dummy. He makes up mind to duck neither too quickly nor too slowly, and declarer will have to guess what to do.

It is usually right to withhold an honour that is safe from capture. If you have K-x-x-x of trumps in front of dummy's A-x-x, you should duck if declarer leads the queen. Barring any 'smother plays' by declarer, your king will always be worth a trick.

However, it would not be so clear to duck the queen if this were a side suit. An inexperienced declarer could be trying a 'Chinese finesse' by leading the unsupported queen!

The following hand, on which West must decline to cover an honour, proves that bridge is a strange game.

Dlr: South
Vul: Both

```
                    ♠ J 4
                    ♡ 8 5 3
                    ◇ A 9 7 5 4 2
                    ♣ J 3
  ♠ 10 9 8 6 5                        ♠ K 3 2
  ♡ Q 9 6                             ♡ J 10 4 2
  ◇ Q 10 6            □               ◇ 8
  ♣ K 8                               ♣ A 10 9 6 5
                    ♠ A Q 7
                    ♡ A K 7
                    ◇ K J 3
                    ♣ Q 7 4 2
```

WEST	NORTH	EAST	SOUTH
			1 ♣
Pass	1 ◇	Pass	2 NT
Pass	3 NT	All Pass	

West's spade lead is covered by the jack, king, and ace. Declarer sees an easy make if diamonds are no worse than 3-1. He cashes the ◇K and leads the jack, planning to duck to preserve communication with dummy. But when West plays the *ten* under the jack, declarer understandably reconsiders He plays the ace from dummy and winds up going down.

Note that if diamonds were in fact 4-0, with West holding Q-10-8-6, West again would need to refrain from covering the jack. This time declarer would take three tricks instead of five.

Problems

1. Dlr: South   ♠ K 10 8 3
     Vul: None   ♡ Q 4 3
                  ◇ 10 6 5 3
                  ♣ A K

♠ A 4
♡ J 10 9 7 5   □
◇ K Q 9
♣ 8 7 6

WEST	NORTH	EAST	SOUTH
			Pass
Pass	1 ◇	Pass	1 NT
All Pass			

You, West, lead the ♡J. Declarer wins the king, partner playing the two. At trick two, declarer leads the ♠J. What do you play?

2. Dlr: North   ♠ Q J 2
     Vul: N-S   ♡ A 9 3
                  ◇ A 9 4
                  ♣ K 6 5 3

♠ 8 6
♡ K Q 6 2   □
◇ 10 6 5 3
♣ Q J 10

WEST	NORTH	EAST	SOUTH
	1 ♣	Pass	1 ♠
Pass	1 NT	Pass	2 ♡
Pass	3 ♠	Pass	4 ♠
All Pass			

You, West, lead the ♣Q, which holds. The ♣J also wins, but declarer ruffs the third club. At trick four, declarer leads the ♡J. Do you cover?

Solutions

1. Win the ace. It is often right to duck in this position, giving declarer a chance to misguess if partner holds the queen, but that is a shortsighted view on this deal. If you duck, you will have to play your ace 'on air' the next time declarer leads a spade toward dummy, and if partner holds Q-9-7-x-x, declarer will take two tricks when he only deserves one. The full deal:

```
                    ♠ K 10 8 3
                    ♡ Q 4 3
                    ◇ 10 6 5 3
                    ♣ A K
    ♠ A 4                            ♠ Q 9 7 5 2
    ♡ J 10 9 7 5                     ♡ 8 2
    ◇ K Q 9         □               ◇ A J 8
    ♣ 8 7 6                          ♣ Q 10 9
                    ♠ J 6
                    ♡ A K 6
                    ◇ 7 4 2
                    ♣ J 5 4 3 2
```

South could always make the contract by attacking clubs, but the line of play he chose was reasonable.

2. With no good intermediates in hearts, and with declarer known to have length in the suit, you certainly should duck. The full deal:

```
                    ♠ Q J 2
                    ♡ A 9 3
                    ◇ A 9 4
                    ♣ K 6 5 3
    ♠ 8 6                            ♠ 9 5 3
    ♡ K Q 6 2                        ♡ 4
    ◇ 10 6 5 3      □               ◇ K J 8 7 2
    ♣ Q J 10                         ♣ A 9 8 7
                    ♠ A K 10 7 4
                    ♡ J 10 8 7 5
                    ◇ Q
                    ♣ 4 2
```

If you cover, declarer wins the ace, draws trumps, knocks out your other heart, and claims, making four. But see what happens if you duck. Declarer must draw trumps to avoid conceding a heart ruff, and this leaves him with just one trump. You will duck again when declarer leads a second heart. He can win the nine and ace, but he lacks the entries to set up his fifth heart and will be held to nine tricks.

Incidentally, the contract would be cold if dummy had the ◇10 instead of you.

Problems

3. Dlr: East   ♠ 10 7
    Vul: None   ♡ 7 6
                 ◇ A J 10 9 4 2
                 ♣ J 6 4

                              ♠ Q 8 6 3 2
                              ♡ 10 4
                 □   ◇ K Q 6 3
                              ♣ K 2

WEST	NORTH	EAST	SOUTH
		Pass	1 ♡
Pass	1 NT	Pass	3 ♣
Pass	3 ◇	Dbl	3 ♠
Pass	4 ♣	Pass	5 ♣
All Pass			

West, your partner, leads the ♣3, and declarer calls for dummy's jack. Do you cover?

4. Dlr: North   ♠ J 5
    Vul: N-S   ♡ A K 6 5 4
                 ♡ A 6 5 4
                 ♣ J 10

                              ♠ Q 9 4
                              ♡ Q J 10 7
                 □   ◇ J 7 2
                              ♣ Q 9 7

WEST	NORTH	EAST	SOUTH
	1 ♡	Pass	2 ♣
Pass	2 ◇	Pass	3 NT
All Pass			

West, your partner, leads the ♠6. You cover dummy's jack, and declarer plays low. Partner overtakes your ♠9 with the ten at trick two, and continues with the eight, driving out declarer's ace. Declarer goes to the ♡A and leads the ♣J. Do you cover?

Solutions

3.
```
                   ♠ 10 7
                   ♡ 7 6
                   ♢ A J 10 9 4 2
                   ♣ J 6 4
  ♠ A 9 4                          ♠ Q 8 6 3 2
  ♡ Q J 8 5          □             ♡ 10 4
  ♢ 8 7 5                          ♢ K Q 6 3
  ♣ 8 7 3                          ♣ K 2
                   ♠ K J 5
                   ♡ A K 9 3 2
                   ♢ –
                   ♣ A Q 10 9 5
```

This deal comes from the 1969 Bermuda Bowl. It was a bad year for the U.S. team, which struggled to finish third, but the United States gained here. At one table, Brazil went down in 3♢ on the N-S cards. In the replay, the U.S. pair bid as shown. On the trump lead, East unwisely *covered* the ♣J with his king.

Declarer won the ace, cashed the top hearts and successfully ruffed a heart with the ♣4. A spade went on the ♢A, a diamond was ruffed, and declarer ruffed another heart with the ♣6. Another diamond ruff put him back in hand to draw trumps and cash the good heart. He lost two spades at the finish but made his contract.

If East had refrained from covering the ♣J, the result would probably have been two down. And indeed, there was nothing to gain by covering and plenty to lose.

This problem really belongs in Quiz 4.

4.

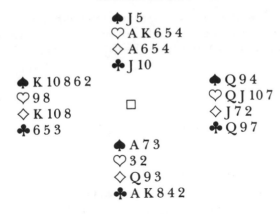

You should cover to block the club suit. If you duck, declarer will let the ♣J ride and will wind up with five clubs, two hearts, a diamond, and a spade. However, if you cover, declarer is tangled up and can't reach his hand to take all his clubs. Whether he ducks your ♣Q or wins, returns to the ♣10 and tries a diamond, the contract will fail.

Quiz 4

Third-Hand Play

As third hand, you tend to play *high*. By sacrificing a high card, you force declarer to spend one of *his* high cards to win the trick, and you may promote some of your side's intermediates.

$$\heartsuit 8\,4\,2$$
$$\heartsuit Q\,10\,6\,3 \qquad \square \qquad \heartsuit K\,9\,5$$
$$\heartsuit A\,J\,7$$

When West leads the ♡3, East must play the king. Declarer wins the ace, and now West's queen and ten are worth two tricks behind declarer's jack. But if East plays a cowardly nine on partner's lead, declarer will win a thoroughly undeserved trick with the jack.

The idea of 'third hand high' has many exceptions. *If there is no prospect of gain by putting up a high card in third seat, you are by no means obligated to play it.*

$$\spadesuit Q\,7\,4$$
$$\square \qquad \spadesuit K\,10\,2$$

Hearts are trumps, your partner's opening lead is the ♠3, and dummy plays the four. You know that declarer has the ♠A, so it can't be right to play the king. Finesse your ten, hoping partner led from the jack.

If your holding were K-9-2, you would play the nine. So long as declarer is known to have the ace, you withhold your king.

$$\spadesuit A\,10\,5$$
$$\square \qquad \spadesuit J\,8\,4$$

Partner leads the two, and dummy contributes the five. West doubtless would have led the king if he had both king and queen, so declarer is marked with at least one honour. Therefore, try the eight, saving a trick if the situation is:

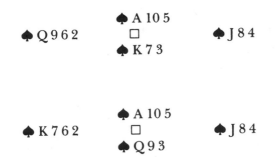

♠ A 10 5
♠ Q 9 6 2   □   ♠ J 8 4
♠ K 7 3

or:

♠ A 10 5
♠ K 7 6 2   □   ♠ J 8 4
♠ Q 9 3

There is a special consideration if you are third to play with two or more *equal* high cards. In such a case, play the *cheapest* one. This is intended to help tell your partner what you have.

765
K 8 4 2   □   Q J 10
A 9 3

West leads the two of this suit. East, with a choice of equal honours to play from, correctly puts up the *ten*. When this forces declarer's ace, West can tell that his partner has the queen and jack as well. Note that if East mistakenly plays the queen, West will have no idea where the missing honours are after declarer's ace wins.

7
K 9 6 4 2   □   A J 3
Q 10 8 5

West, who is known from the bidding to have a weak hand (probably without a side entry), leads this suit against a no-trump contract. If East wins the ace and returns the jack, declarer can *duck* and limit the defence to three tricks. Declarer could also duck effectively if East astutely played the *jack* at trick one, but very few players would do so – South might wind up with no tricks at all if West had A-K-9-4-2.

Sometimes a really deep finesse by third hand is worth considering.

```
                    J 8
  K 7 5 2           ☐              A 9 4
                  Q 10 6 3
```

Partner leads the two against a no-trump contract, and dummy plays the eight. With declarer known to have four cards in this suit, including at least one honour (partner would not lead low from K-Q-10-2), East might well play the nine. Now E-W will end with three tricks instead of two. Note, however, that East would have to grab the ace if he were defending a *suit* contract.

```
                    J 5
  A 9 8 4 2         ☐              Q 7 6
                  K 10 3
```

West leads the four vs. no-trump. If dummy plays low, the six from East would save a trick!

```
                    9 2
  A 7 4 3           ☐              J 8 5
                  K Q 10 6
```

West leads the three against no-trump, and East can save a trick by playing the eight on dummy's two.

Third hand must be alert at all times. For example, it may be necessary to unblock a suit.

```
Dlr: South              ♠ A 6
Vul: N-S                ♡ 7 6 4
                        ◇ A J 7 3
                        ♣ Q J 6 2
    ♠ K J 9 5 3                        ♠ Q 8
    ♡ K 5 2                            ♡ Q J 10 9 3
    ◇ 8 6 2            ☐              ◇ K 9 5
    ♣ 9 8                             ♣ 7 5 4
                        ♠ 10 7 4 2
                        ♡ A 8
                        ◇ Q 10 4
                        ♣ A K 10 3
```

WEST	NORTH	EAST	SOUTH
			1 ♣
Pass	3 ♣	Pass	3 NT
All Pass			

West leads the ♠5. Declarer is afraid of a possible heart switch, and he sees a chance to block the spade suit anyway, so he rises with the ace. To defeat the contract, East must get his ♠Q out of partner's way, a play that is never likely to cost.

Would you play 'third hand high' as East on this deal?

```
Dlr: South            ♠ Q 3 2
Vul: N-S              ♡ K 8 7
                      ◇ J 9 8
                      ♣ 10 8 7 6
    ♠ 10 5                           ♠ 7 6
    ♡ J 9 3 2                        ♡ A Q 10 4
    ◇ A 7 6 4 3 2      □             ◇ Q 10 5
    ♣ 2                              ♣ Q J 5 3
                      ♠ A K J 9 8 4
                      ♡ 6 5
                      ◇ K
                      ♣ A K 9 4
```

WEST	NORTH	EAST	SOUTH
			1 ♠
Pass	1 NT	Pass	2 ♣
Pass	2 ♠	Pass	4 ♠
All Pass			

West chooses the doubtful lead of a club. If East puts up an honour, declarer wins, draws trumps with the ace and queen, and finesses in clubs to pick up the whole suit.

West's lead is marked by the bidding as a singleton, so East should realize that sacrificing an honour can't gain anything. Notice the difference if he plays low on the first trick. South wins cheaply in dummy, but he can't lead another club – West will ruff. Instead, declarer must draw trumps. Now, lacking a second entry to dummy, he must lose a club trick.

Problems

1.   Dlr: South   ♠ J 10 3
      Vul: N-S   ♡ J 4
                  ◇ K Q 10 6 4
                  ♣ 7 6 5

                                ♠ K 8
                                ♡ K 9 8 7
                 □   ◇ A 5 3
                                ♣ J 10 9 8

WEST	NORTH	EAST	SOUTH
			1 ♣
Pass	1 ◇	Pass	2 NT
Pass	3 NT	All Pass	

West, your partner, leads the ♣5, and dummy contributes the jack. What do you play and why?

2.   Dlr: North   ♠ J 7 3
      Vul: None   ♡ A 4 3
                  ◇ J 9 3
                  ♣ Q 9 8 4

                                ♠ 9 5 2
                                ♡ J 9
                 □   ◇ A K 5 2
                                ♣ K J 6 2

WEST	NORTH	EAST	SOUTH
	Pass	1 ♣	1 NT
Pass	2 NT	Pass	3 NT
All Pass			

West, your partner, leads the ♣7. Plan your defence.

Solutions

1.   Play low. This will cost nothing in the long run – declarer is marked with an honour, so he is entitled to at least one spade trick. You may gain heavily, though, if you can deny declarer a late entry to the diamond suit.

```
            ♠ J 10 3
            ♡ J 4
            ◇ K Q 10 6 4
            ♣ 7 6 5
♠ Q 9 6 5 2              ♠ K 8
♡ Q 6 5                 ♡ K 9 8 7
◇ 8 7 2        □        ◇ A 5 3
♣ 4 3                  ♣ J 10 9 8
            ♠ A 7 4
            ♡ A 10 3 2
            ◇ J 9
            ♣ A K Q 2
```

If you put up the ♠K, declarer will win the ace and force out your ◇A. Now no matter what you return, declarer has time to reach dummy with the ♠10 to cash the diamonds.

Note the difference if you duck. Declarer is held to three clubs, one diamond (West will give count when declarer leads a diamond, allowing you to win your ace at the right time), two hearts, and two spades.

Notice that you would never defeat the contract if West had five spades to the *ace* and no ♡Q.

2. Partner's lead marks him with two or three small clubs, so it will benefit only declarer if you play the jack.

```
            ♠ J 7 3
            ♡ A 4 3
            ◇ J 9 3
            ♣ Q 9 8 4
♠ K 10 6 4              ♠ 9 5 2
♡ 10 8 7 6             ♡ J 9
◇ 6 4          □        ◇ A K 5 2
♣ 7 5 3                ♣ K J 6 2
            ♠ A Q 8
            ♡ K Q 5 2
            ◇ Q 10 8 7
            ♣ A 10
```

When declarer wins the ♣10, he can succeed double-dummy by leading the ♠Q at trick two. If South is made of flesh and blood, down one is much more likely.

Problems

3. Dlr: South   ♠ J 4
    Vul: None   ♡ A J 8 3
                      ◇ A K Q 9 6
                      ♣ 9 5
                                          ♠ A 9 7 2
                                          ♡ Q 4 2
                      ☐   ◇ J
                                          ♣ A K Q 7 4

WEST	NORTH	EAST	SOUTH
			Pass
Pass	1 ◇	Dbl	1 ♠
Pass	1 NT	2 ♣	2 ♣
3 ♣	4 ♠	All Pass	

West, your partner, leads the ♣J. Plan your defence.

4. Dlr: South   ♠ A 10 3
    Vul: None   ♡ 7 6 5
                      ◇ Q 9 2
                      ♣ K J 4 3
                                          ♠ 8 6 2
                                          ♡ Q 10 8 2
                      ☐   ◇ 4 3
                                          ♣ 10 8 6 5

WEST	NORTH	EAST	SOUTH
			1 NT[1]
Pass	3 NT	All Pass	

[1] 15-17 HCP

West, your partner, leads the ♠5 and dummy plays low. Plan
your defence.

Solutions

3.

```
                    ♠ J 4
                    ♡ A J 8 3
                    ◇ A K Q 9 6
                    ♣ 9 5
   ♠ 5                           ♠ A 9 7 2
   ♡ 10 7 5                      ♡ Q 4 2
   ◇ 10 7 5 4 2      □           ◇ J
   ♣ J 10 8 6                    ♣ A K Q 7 4
                    ♠ K Q 10 8 6 3
                    ♡ K 9 6
                    ◇ 8 3
                    ♣ 3 2
```

The deal is from the 1967 Bermuda Bowl final, United States vs. Italy. When the Italians were E-W, East, Walter Averelli, overtook the ♣J at trick one and shifted to the ◇J. He won the first trump lead, underled in clubs to Giorgio Belladonna's ten, and took a diamond ruff for the setting trick.

A gain for the Italians? No – 4♠ was reached in the replay, and Edgar Kaplan and Norman Kay, E-W for the United States, defeated the contract in exactly the same way.

4.

```
                    ♠ A 10 3
                    ♡ 7 6 5
                    ◇ Q 9 2
                    ♣ K J 4 3
   ♠ K J 7 5 4                   ♠ 8 6 2
   ♡ J 9 3                       ♡ Q 10 8 2
   ◇ A 8 6         □             ◇ 4 3
   ♣ A 7                         ♣ 10 8 6 5
                    ♠ Q 9
                    ♡ A K 4
                    ◇ K J 10 7 5
                    ♣ Q 9 2
```

You should play the *two*. It is more important to give partner the count, especially when you have such a bad hand, than to make a nominal contribution to the trick.

After winning the first trick, declarer will knock out partner's ◇A. What should West do now? It's easy to lead the ♠K when looking at all four hands. But if the South hand were

♠ Q 9 6
♡ A K Q
♢ K J 10 3
♣ 10 6 5,

West needs to lead a low club, or anything but another spade. If East plays his ♠2 on the opening lead, though, West has an easy time avoiding a losing play.

Quiz 5

Using the Rule of Eleven

Let us look again at a situation that was touched upon in the quiz on third-hand play:

♠ J 8 6
□   ♠ K 9 4

West leads the ♠5 against a 4♡ contract, and dummy plays the six. It was suggested that East withhold his king and try the nine instead. But on the assumption that partner's lead is his fourth-best spade, *you can be sure that the nine will force the ace.* Think about it. Partner has three spades that outrank the five, and they must be the queen, ten, and seven since those are the only three spades higher than the five that aren't in view (besides the ace that declarer must hold).

In lieu of working out partner's holding, you may use a shortcut known as *the Rule of Eleven.*

Assuming that partner has led fourth highest, you can subtract his spot card value from eleven. The remainder yields the number of higher-ranking cards held by the other three hands.

Applying the Rule to the example we just saw;

                    J 8 6
5 led >>>   □   K 9 4

Subtract West's spot card, the five, from eleven, leaving a remainder of six. So in your hand, declarer's hand and the dummy, there are six cards higher than the five. You can see five of these – six, eight, nine, jack, and king. So declarer has only one card higher than the five, and it must be the ace.

Some people find all this a little mysterious, and textbooks usually decline to elaborate, so perhaps it would be well to explain further. Consider a suit of thirteen cards:

A K Q J 10 9 8 7 6 5 4 3 2

Now assign appropriate number values to the honours.

A K Q J
14 13 12 11 10 9 8 7 6 5 4 3 2

When somebody leads a fourth-best spot card, three other higher cards are accounted for. In effect, 'eleven' becomes the highest-ranking card remaining.

~~14~~ ~~13~~ ~~12~~ 11 10 9 8 7 6 5 4 3 2

Of these remaining cards, the ones that rank above leader's spot card are held by the other three players. Therefore, their number may be obtained by simply subtracting leader's spot card from eleven. That's as simple as I can make it.

The following quiz illustrates a variety of situations in which the Rule of Eleven may be helpful.

Problems

1. Dlr: South
   Vul: None

                    ♠ A J 7 3
                    ♡ A K Q 3
                    ◇ K 5 3
                    ♣ Q 4

                                    ♠ 10 8 2
                                    ♡ J 9 4
          7♦   □   ◇ A J 9 2
          Lead   ♣ K 10 5

WEST	NORTH	EAST	SOUTH
			Pass
Pass	1 ◇	Pass	1 NT
Pass	3 NT	All Pass	

West, your partner, leads the ◇7 and dummy plays low. Which diamond do you play?

2. Dlr: South
Vul: Both

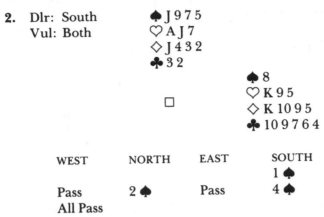

♠ J 9 7 5
♡ A J 7
◇ J 4 3 2
♣ 3 2

♠ 8
♡ K 9 5
◇ K 10 9 5
♣ 10 9 7 6 4

WEST	NORTH	EAST	SOUTH
			1 ♠
Pass	2 ♠	Pass	4 ♠
All Pass			

West, your partner, leads the ♡6 and dummy plays the seven. How do you defend?

Solutions

1.

♠ A J 7 3
♡ A K Q 3
◇ K 5 3
♣ Q 4

♠ Q 9 4
♡ 10 8 5
◇ Q 10 8 7 4
♣ 8 7

♠ 10 8 2
♡ J 9 4
◇ A J 9 2
♣ K 10 5

♠ K 6 5
♡ 7 6 2
◇ 6
♣ A J 9 6 3 2

The Rule of Eleven reveals that declarer has no diamond that can beat the seven (eleven minus seven equals four; dummy has the king, you have the nine, jack, and ace). So you can play your two, letting partner hold the lead to come through dummy again. If you play any other diamond, the contract will make.

2. Applying the Rule of Eleven, we learn that declarer has no cards higher than the six. So the nine is good enough to win the trick. The full deal:

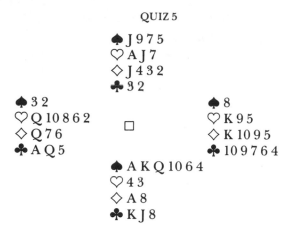

```
              ♠ J 9 7 5
              ♡ A J 7
              ◇ J 4 3 2
              ♣ 3 2
♠ 3 2                              ♠ 8
♡ Q 10 8 6 2        □             ♡ K 9 5
◇ Q 7 6                            ◇ K 10 9 5
♣ A Q 5                            ♣ 10 9 7 6 4
              ♠ A K Q 10 6 4
              ♡ 4 3
              ◇ A 8
              ♣ K J 8
```

Inaccurate defence would be costly this time. If East puts up his ♡K, declarer will finesse the ♡J later, obtain a discard for his diamond loser, and make the contract.

Problems

3. Dlr: South   ♠ J 10
   Vul: N-S   ♡ A K
                      ◇ Q J 9 3 2
                      ♣ K 4 3 2

   ♠ Q 7 2
   ♡ 7 6 5 4
   ◇ K 6   □
   ♣ A 10 7 6

WEST	NORTH	EAST	SOUTH
			Pass
Pass	1 ◇	Pass	1 ♡
Pass	2 ♣	Pass	2 NT
Pass	3 NT	All Pass	

You, West, choose the unbid suit to lead against 3 NT. Partner produces the ♠A, and declarer follows with the four. Partner returns the ♠6 to declarer's king. What do you play and why?

4. Dlr: South   ♠ K 6 3
   Vul: None   ♡ J 5 3
              ◇ 9 8
              ♣ K Q 10 6 4

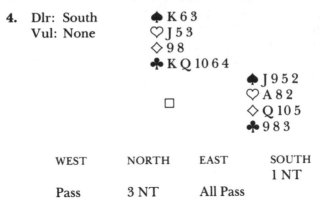

                              ♠ J 9 5 2
                              ♡ A 8 2
                              ◇ Q 10 5
                              ♣ 9 8 3

WEST	NORTH	EAST	SOUTH
			1 NT
Pass	3 NT	All Pass	

West, your partner, leads the six of diamonds – eight, queen, king. Declarer continues with a club to dummy's king, winning, and leads the jack of hearts. What do you play and why?

Solutions

3. You can employ the Rule of Eleven *when your partner returns the lead of your suit* – if you know his card is his original fourth highest in the suit.

                    ♠ J 10
                    ♡ A K
                    ◇ Q J 9 3 2
                    ♣ K 4 3 2

♠ Q 7 2   ♠ A 9 8 6 3
♡ 7 6 5 4   ♡ 10 8
◇ K 6   □   ◇ 8 7 5
♣ A 10 7 6   ♣ Q J 8

                    ♠ K 5 4
                    ♡ Q J 9 3 2
                    ◇ A 10 4
                    ♣ 9 5

Declarer wins the second spade because he suspects that the spades are 4-4, and he fears a club switch anyway. West must be careful. If East's ♠6 is his original fourth-best spade (and on the bidding, it can hardly be otherwise), the Rule of Eleven applies – it indicates that declarer has no spade left that is higher than the six. So West can safely unblock his ♠Q under the king. When West wins his ◇K, the defenders will be able to take all their spade tricks.

4. On the Rule of Eleven, declarer's ◇K was the only one he had higher than partner's six, so partner's suit is ready to run. Since West is a heavy favourite to have at least five diamonds (where are all the lower spot cards?), rise with the ♡A and fire back a diamond.

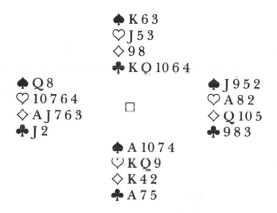

Declarer was faking a finesse when he led that ♡J, trying to steal his ninth trick.

Quiz 6

Full Circle: Fourth-Hand Play

This may seem like an odd subject for a Quiz. What problems could the defender who is *last* to play have? After all, fourth hand is well placed – he can see what everybody else has put on the trick before committing himself. In fact, there are more subtleties in defenders' play here than in any other seat.

Fourth hand has frequent opportunities for *deceptive* play. This topic is covered in depth in Quiz 23, so only one or two illustrations will be given here:

```
                 A K 8 3
   Q 4             □           10 9 5
                 J 7 6 2
```

This suit is trumps, and declarer begins by leading low to the king. If East plays the five, declarer will have no choice but to cash the ace next, dropping West's queen. But if East follows with the nine or ten on the first lead, declarer has the losing option of returning to hand and leading the jack, trying to pin the 10-9 doubleton.

```
                 10 4
   8 7 2           □           K J 9 3
                 A Q 6 5
```

This is a side suit. Declarer leads low to the queen and cashes the ace. If East follows with the three and nine, declarer knows he can ruff his small cards in dummy without fear of an overruff. But if East gives away no additional information by dropping the king on the second lead, declarer may have to worry about being overruffed.

$\heartsuit$ 6

$\heartsuit$ A 4 3   □ $\heartsuit$ J 7

$\heartsuit$ K Q 10 9 8 5 2

Declarer, having opened 3$\heartsuit$, plays in 4$\heartsuit$. He wins the opening lead in dummy and plays a heart to his king. Unless there is some compelling reason to win, West should duck. If declarer has all the hearts, it hardly matters whether West wins or ducks; but if East started with J-x, West *must* duck to offer declarer an option. This is hardly the greatest play ever made – it's just routine technique that gives declarer a chance to go wrong.

Q J 10 9

K 7 5   □   8 6 2

A 4 3

Declarer leads the queen of this suit. West can make declarer's communications a little less fluid by allowing the first finesse to work.

Sometimes, refusing to take a winner will gain a trick by force.

$\spadesuit$ K Q 6 5 2
$\heartsuit$ 10 5 4 3
$\diamondsuit$ 6 5
$\clubsuit$ K 5

$\spadesuit$ 8 7 4 3
$\heartsuit$ J
$\diamondsuit$ A J 7 4 3   □
$\clubsuit$ 10 9 7

$\spadesuit$ A 10 9
$\heartsuit$ Q 9 8
$\diamondsuit$ K 10 8
$\clubsuit$ J 8 4 3

$\spadesuit$ J
$\heartsuit$ A K 7 6 2
$\diamondsuit$ Q 9 2
$\clubsuit$ A Q 6 2

In a matchpoint duplicate game, South plays in 4$\heartsuit$ and receives a helpful club lead, won by the king. Playing for the maximum, declarer cashes the $\heartsuit$AK and follows with two more high clubs, discarding a diamond from dummy. Now the $\spadesuit$J is led, West playing the eight.

If East wins, he can do no better than cash his high trump and a diamond. Declarer easily takes four heart tricks, three clubs, one ruff in dummy, and *two* spades for ten tricks. But East knows that declarer, while he doesn't have four quick losers, is looking for winners. So East ducks, and declarer has to end up a trick short.

(If East had one club less and one spade more, the contract still could be made. After winning the ♠J, declarer could lead his fourth club and discard dummy's last diamond. East would have no way to get in to cash his high trump, and declarer could ruff two diamonds in dummy, losing only one diamond, one heart and one club!)

On the last deal, fourth hand's refusal to take a winner costs a trick but gains one that is more important.

Dlr: South
Vul: N-S

	♠ J 4	
	♡ 8 5 3	
	◇ Q 7 5 4 2	
	♣ J 5 3	
♠ Q 10 8 2		♠ 9 6 5
♡ K 10 2		♡ Q 9 7 4
◇ A J 10		◇ 9 6
♣ 8 7 4		♣ Q 10 9 2
	♠ A K 7 3	
	♡ A J 6	
	◇ K 8 3	
	♣ A K 6	

South opens 2NT, and North raises hopefully to 3 NT. West's spade lead looks poor when dummy's jack wins, but in fact declarer has just lost his late entry to dummy. Suppose he leads a low diamond to the nine and king at trick two. If West grabs this trick, preserving his second stopper, declarer will win the return, duck a diamond, and take three diamonds, three spades, two clubs, and a heart.

The difference is striking if West smoothly withholds the ◇A. Declarer could, in theory, continue with a diamond to the king. Although the long diamonds are now dead, he can salvage an eighth trick for down one. In practice, declarer will duck the second diamond in dummy, playing East for A-9 doubleton, and now he should finish down two.

Problems

1. Dlr: South
    Vul: Nonc

    ♠ K Q 4 3
    ♡ J 10
    ♢ J 10 4 3
    ♣ A Q 4

    ♠ A J 9 2
    ♡ K 8 7 6 2
    ♢ 7 6
    ♣ 5 2

WEST	NORTH	EAST	SOUTH
			1 ♣
Pass	1 ♠	Pass	2 NT
Pass	4 NT	Pass	6 NT
All Pass			

West, your partner, leads the ♢9. Plan your defence.

2. Dlr: South
    Vul: N-S

    ♣ 8 5
    ♡ Q 6 4
    ♢ K Q 8 7 6 5
    ♣ 7 6

    ♠ J 9 8 4
    ♡ 8 5
    ♢ A J 10
    ♣ K 10 9 8

South opened 2 NT and converted partner's 3♢ response to
3 NT. West, your partner, leads the ♡J, won by declarer's king.
The ♢2 is led to West's four and dummy's king. Plan your
defence.

Solutions

1.
$$\spadesuit\ K\ Q\ 4\ 3$$
$$\heartsuit\ J\ 10$$
$$\diamondsuit\ J\ 10\ 4\ 3$$
$$\clubsuit\ A\ Q\ 4$$

♠ 10 8 5	♠ A J 9 2
♡ 5 4 3	♡ K 8 7 6 2
◇ 9 8 5 2 □	◇ 7 6
♣ 9 8 7	♣ 5 2

$$\spadesuit\ 7\ 6$$
$$\heartsuit\ A\ Q\ 9$$
$$\diamondsuit\ A\ K\ Q$$
$$\clubsuit\ K\ J\ 10\ 6\ 3$$

When declarer plays the inevitable spade to dummy's queen, East must duck without batting an eyelid. Suppose, instead, that he wins and returns a diamond. Since declarer has only one spade trick, he must take the heart finesse and will make his contract. But what if the ♠Q holds? Now declarer is left in the dark. Should he try a heart to the queen or lead up to the ♠K?

East knows on the bidding that declarer has the ♡A and ♡Q, so he must not force declarer to take the heart finesse that he knows will win.

2.
$$\spadesuit\ 6\ 5$$
$$\heartsuit\ Q\ 6\ 4$$
$$\diamondsuit\ K\ Q\ 8\ 7\ 6\ 5$$
$$\clubsuit\ 7\ 6$$

♠ 10 7 3 2	♠ J 9 8 4
♡ J 10 9 7 2	♡ 8 5
◇ 4 3 □	◇ A J 10
♣ Q 5	♣ K 10 9 8

$$\spadesuit\ A\ K\ Q$$
$$\heartsuit\ A\ K\ 3$$
$$\diamondsuit\ 9\ 2$$
$$\clubsuit\ A\ J\ 4\ 3\ 2$$

If East wins the first diamond and returns, say, a heart, declarer wins in hand, leads a diamond to the queen, concedes a diamond, and claims the rest. But note the effect if East has the elementary technique to duck the first diamond. In effect, this costs declarer an entry he needs to set up the suit, and eight tricks will be the limit.

Declarer's play, while all right at matchpoints, would be wrong at IMPs or rubber bridge. On the first round of diamonds it would be correct to play small from both hands! The contract is unbeatable on this line, assuming a 3-2 diamond break.

Suppose that the lie of the diamond suit is:

```
        K Q 10 8 5 3
7 6         □          A J 2
        9 4
```

Declarer astutely leads the ◇9 and plays low from the dummy. If East wins the jack, the contract will be made. An expert East would play low! Now declarer still has a chance to go down – he might continue by leading a diamond to the ten, playing West for A-J-7-6.

Problems

3. Dlr: West   ♠ K 4
    Vul: None   ♡ 9 6 3
                ◇ A 7 5 2
                ♣ A K 8 4

                        ♠ Q 10 3
                        ♡ Q 7
            □   ◇ Q 9 3
                        ♣ Q J 9 7 2

WEST	NORTH	EAST	SOUTH
Pass	1 ◇	Pass	1 ♠
Pass	2 ♣	Pass	2 NT
Pass	3 NT	All Pass	

West, your partner, leads the ♡5. Declarer ducks your queen, ducks again to partner's jack when you return the suit, and wins his ace on the third round as you discard a club. Next comes a spade to the king. Plan your defence.

4. Dlr: South
    Vul: N-S

          ♠ 7 5
          ♡ K J 2
          ◇ A 7 6 3
          ♣ K J 9 4

                      ♠ K 10 6 2
              □   ♡ 7 6
                      ◇ Q 10 5
                      ♣ A 7 6 3

WEST	NORTH	EAST	SOUTH
			1 ♡
Pass	2 ♣	Pass	2 NT
Pass	3 ♡	Pass	4 ♡
All Pass			

West, your partner, leads a low trump, won by declarer's eight.
Declarer considers briefly, then leads the ♣10. Partner plays the
eight and dummy the four. How do you defend?

Solutions

3.

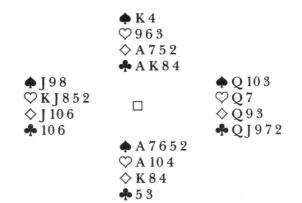

To beat the contract, East must throw his ♠Q under dummy's
king. If declarer's spades are as good as A-J-x-x-x, the ♠Q is a
doomed card anyway. But if declarer A-x-x-x-x and East hangs
on to the queen, declarer always can set up four spade tricks
(and nine in all) without letting West in to cash his two good
hearts. Work it out for yourself.

4.

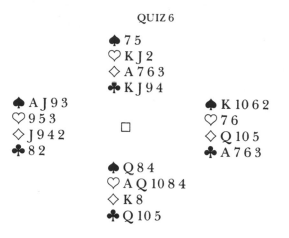

```
              ♠ 7 5
              ♡ K J 2
              ◇ A 7 6 3
              ♣ K J 9 4
♠ A J 9 3                    ♠ K 10 6 2
♡ 9 5 3                      ♡ 7 6
◇ J 9 4 2      □             ◇ Q 10 5
♣ 8 2                        ♣ A 7 6 3
              ♠ Q 8 4
              ♡ A Q 10 8 4
              ◇ K 8
              ♣ Q 10 5
```

Why has declarer not drawn trumps? He must have three bad spades and can't afford to take out all of dummy's trumps until he dislodges the ♣A. Assuming declarer has not rebid 2 NT with a singleton club, West's ♣8 indicates a doubleton. Therefore, you should duck the first club – this renders declarer helpless. If he draws no more than two trumps and then leads a second club, you win and give West a ruff. If declarer draws all the trumps, the defence has three spade tricks to take when you win the ♣A.

Quiz 7

Later Leads

Generally, picking a suit to lead is the hardest part of first-hand play – once you decide on a suit, the card you lead from that suit is a matter of convention. However, very little in bridge is true a hundred percent of the time, and some imagination in choosing a lead may be called for, especially in the middle or late stages of the play.

In this Quiz, we will deal with some offbeat leads in the area of *tactics*. Leads that involve a fine point of *technique* are dealt with in Quiz 18.

Normally, you lead the top card in a sequence to prevent declarer from winning a cheap trick. However:

```
                    ♠ K 6
                    ♡ A J 10 6 4
                    ◇ J 6 4
                    ♣ K 7 6
  ♠ J 10 8 3                        ♠ A 9 4 2
  ♡ 9 5 2                           ♡ 8 7 3
  ◇ A 9            □               ◇ K Q 10 7
  ♣ 9 8 5 4                         ♣ J 3
                    ♠ Q 7 5
                    ♡ K Q
                    ◇ 8 5 3 2
                    ♣ A Q 10 2
```

WEST	NORTH	EAST	SOUTH
			1 ♣
Pass	1 ♡	Pass	1 NT
Pass	3 NT	All Pass	

West leads the ♠J, and dummy plays low. East can hold declarer to one spade trick by ducking here. But declarer's play is suspicious. His normal course would be to try to win the ♠K; if he had Q-x-x in hand, he could preserve a tenace there. Chances are, he would like East to duck because he has nine tricks to cash if he can get in. If East works all this out, he will see that the only chance is to win and shift to the ◇7.

The other side of the coin:

Dlr: North   ♠ A Q 4 3
Vul: E-W   ♡ A K 9 3 2
Matchpoints   ◇ K 4
                   ♣ J 3
                              ♠ 10 7
                   □   ♡ J 10
                              ◇ A 5 3
                              ♣ K Q 10 8 6 2

North opens 1♡ and raises South's 1 NT response to 2 NT, passed out. West leads the ♠5, won by dummy's queen. At trick two, declarer calls for the ◇K, and East takes his ace.

East is afraid declarer's hand is something like:

                   ♠ K 6 2
                   ♡ 8 4
                   ◇ Q J 10 7 2
                   ♣ 9 5 4

in which case the defence must cash out. But if East leads the ♣K, West may be nervous about overtaking – he will place declarer with some club length on the bidding. Perhaps East might get the right message across by leading the ♣Q. He could lead low, of course, but that risks finding declarer with the ♣A instead of the ♠K.

Suppose you want partner in the lead badly for some reason, and your only chance seems to be in hearts, where you have K-Q-J-x-x and dummy has A-x. If you lead the king, dummy will duck – so you must lead low, hoping partner owns the ten.

Next, suppose West is end-played and forced to break this suit:

                   A 10 5
       J 7 2   □   Q 8 6 3
                   K 9 4

If West leads low, declarer will have little choice but to pick up the suit without loss. If West leads the jack, he gives declarer a guess.

Here is a brilliant example of an unconventional way to break a suit, first noted, as far as I know, by Terence Reese.

```
Dlr:  North        ♠ A 7 4
Vul:  None         ♡ J 9
                   ♢ J 10 5
                   ♣ A K J 10 3
♠ Q J 9 5                         ♠ 6 3 2
♡ Q 10 6 4                        ♡ K 8 3
♢ K 6 3        □                  ♢ 8 7 4
♣ 8 5                             ♣ Q 9 6 2
                   ♠ K 10 8
                   ♡ A 7 5 2
                   ♢ A Q 9 2
                   ♣ 7 4
```

WEST	NORTH	EAST	SOUTH
	1 ♣	Pass	1 ♡
Pass	2 ♣	Pass	3 NT
All Pass			

West leads the ♠Q. Declarer takes dummy's ace and loses a diamond finesse to West's king. Suppose West switches to a low heart now – nine, king, ace. A club finesse loses to East, but the defenders can take only two heart tricks.

In an article in the December 1969 issue of *The Bridge World*, Reese noted that West could defeat the contract by shifting to the ♡Q (not an obvious shot, to be sure). Declarer might duck this, wrote Reese, but he would have to win the second heart, lest East set up the fifth defensive trick with a switch back to spades. Now West would remain with the ♡10-6 over declarer's seven.

In fact, declarer could still make the contract by catching West in a strip-squeeze, but the principle is sound. Change the deal slightly:

```
                    ♠ A 7 4
                    ♡ J 3
                    ◇ J 10 5
                    ♣ A Q J 10 3
  ♠ Q J 9 5                          ♠ 6 3 2
  ♡ Q 10 8 4          □             ♡ K 7 6
  ◇ K 6 3                            ◇ 8 7 4 2
  ♣ 8 5                              ♣ K 9 6
                    ♠ K 10 8
                    ♡ A 9 5 2
                    ◇ A Q 9
                    ♣ 7 4 2
```

Now the ♡Q switch wins for the defence. Incidentally, the lead
of the queen also would suffice if declarer's heart holding were
K-9-5-2.

```
Dlr: South           ♠ J 2
Vul: N-S             ♡ K Q 4 3
                     ◇ A 8 3
                     ♣ K 7 5 3
  ♠ 9 7 4 3                         ♠ Q 10 8 5
  ♡ J 10 9 8          □             ♡ 7 6
  ◇ J 7 5 2                         ◇ 10 6 4
  ♣ 2                               ♣ J 10 9 8
                     ♠ A K 6
                     ♡ A 5 2
                     ◇ K Q 9
                     ♣ A Q 6 4
```

WEST	NORTH	EAST	SOUTH
			2 NT
Pass	6 NT	All Pass	

West leads the ♡J. Declarer wins and tests hearts and clubs,
finding that neither suit breaks favourably. After cashing three
diamonds, ending in his hand, he exits with a club to East. Now
East must lead the ♠Q not a low spade, to ensure a second
defensive trick.

Problems

1. Dlr: South   ♠ A 6 5
    Vul: Both   ♡ 10 4
                      ◇ K 6 2
                      ♣ A 10 9 6 3

                                     ♠ K 8
                                     ♡ J 9 3 2
                      □   ◇ Q 10 9 8
                                     ♣ K J 5

WEST	NORTH	EAST	SOUTH
			1 ◇
Pass	1 ♣	Pass	1 NT
Pass	2 NT	All Pass	

West, your partner, leads the ♣4. Dummy ducks, and you take your king, declarer dropping the ten. You return a spade to declarer's queen. The ♣Q is run to your king, and you try a shift to the ◇10. Declarer puts in the jack, which wins. Next declarer passes the ♣8, losing to your jack. What do you lead now?

2. Dlr: South   ♠ 7 6 4
    Vul: N-S   ♡ 5
                      ◇ A Q 4 3
                      ♣ Q 6 5 4 3

    ♠ A J 3
    ♡ Q 10 6 2
    ◇ J 9 6 5   □
    ♣ 10 8

WEST	NORTH	EAST	SOUTH
			1 ♠
Pass	2 ♣	Pass	3 ♠
Pass	4 ♠	All Pass	

You, West, lead the ♡2. Partner wins the ace and returns the ♠2 to declarer's king and your ace. What do you lead to trick three?

Solutions

1. Declarer clearly has eight tricks ready to cash – two spades, three diamonds, and three clubs. Perhaps you should have switched to hearts earlier, but you certainly must do so now. Since three fast tricks are needed, you must lead the jack, hoping that South opened on only 12 HCP, leaving West with A-Q-x of hearts.

```
                    ♠ A 6 5
                    ♡ 10 4
                    ◇ K 6 2
                    ♣ A 10 9 6 3
     ♠ J 9 7 4 3 2                  ♠ K 8
     ♡ A Q 7                        ♡ J 9 3 2
     ◇ 5 4          □                ◇ Q 10 9 8
     ♣ 7 4                          ♣ K J 5
                    ♠ Q 10
                    ♡ K 8 6 5
                    ◇ A J 7 3
                    ♣ Q 8 2
```

2. Partner would not return a trump unless he had dummy's club suit locked up and unless he knew from your fourth-best lead that declarer had heart losers. You, meanwhile, can tell that declarer will take three diamond tricks at most. So your aim should be preventing ruffs. Return a low trump, which should break even at worst. In fact, the full deal is:

```
                    ♠ 7 6 4
                    ♡ 5
                    ◇ A Q 4 3
                    ♣ Q 6 5 4 3
     ♠ A J 3                        ♠ 10 2
     ♡ Q 10 6 2                     ♡ A J 9 4
     ◇ J 9 6 5       □               ◇ 10 8 2
     ♣ 10 8                         ♣ K J 9 7
                    ♠ K Q 9 8 5
                    ♡ K 8 7 3
                    ◇ K 7
                    ♣ A 2
```

Had partner wasted his ♠10 by yielding to the reflex of leading the top of a doubleton, the contract would be made. As it is, declarer is a trick short.

Problems

3.   Dlr: North   ♠ K 10 7 5 3
      Vul: None   ♡ J 10 5
                    ◇ 7
                    ♣ A J 10 4

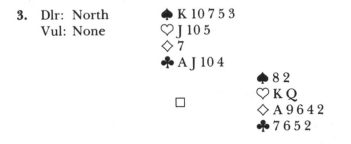

                                 ♠ 8 2
                                 ♡ K Q
                                 ◇ A 9 6 4 2
                                 ♣ 7 6 5 2

South's third-seat 1♠ opening is raised to 4♠ by North, and all pass. West, your partner, leads the ◇Q. How do you defend?

4.   Dlr: South   ♠ A J 6 3
      Vul: E-W   ♡ K 7 6
                    ◇ 8 7 5
                    ♣ J 5 3

♠ 9 8
♡ J 8 5 2
◇ K Q J 9 6   □
♣ 10 7

WEST	NORTH	EAST	SOUTH
			1 NT
Pass	2 ♣	Pass	2 ◇
Pass	2 NT	Pass	3 NT
All Pass			

You, West, lead a hopeful ◇K. Partner plays the four, and declarer the two. What do you lead at trick two?

Solutions

3.   You must play partner for the ♡A. But if you lead the ♡K and continue with the queen, West will play low, waiting for the

third round. Grab partner's attention by leading the ♡Q, then
the king. A good partner will realize the significance of your
unusual play, overtake, and give you a ruff.

```
                    ♠ K 10 7 5 3
                    ♡ J 10 5
                    ◇ 7
                    ♣ A J 10 4
    ♠ 9                              ♠ 8 2
    ♡ A 9 6 2              □         ♡ K Q
    ◇ Q J 10 5                       ◇ A 9 6 4 2
    ♣ Q 9 8 3                        ♣ 7 6 5 2
                    ♠ A Q J 6 4
                    ♡ 8 7 4 3
                    ◇ K 8 3
                    ♣ K
```

4.
```
                    ♠ A J 6 3
                    ♡ K 7 6
                    ◇ 8 7 5
                    ♣ J 5 3
    ♠ 9 8                            ♠ K 10 7 2
    ♡ J 8 5 2             □          ♡ 10 9 4
    ◇ K Q J 9 6                      ◇ A 4 3
    ♣ 10 7                           ♣ 9 6 4
                    ♠ Q 5 4
                    ♡ A Q 3
                    ◇ 10 2
                    ♣ A K Q 8 2
```

It looks as though there could be no problem here, but West
managed to invent one when he carelessly continued with the
◇Q at trick two. East pondered this card for quite a while. It was
not impossible for declarer to have

```
                    ♠ Q x
                    ♡ A Q J
                    ◇ J 10 x x
                    ♣ A K x x,
```

in which case overtaking the second diamond would give

declarer an extra diamond trick and his contract. After much agonized thought, East guessed right, playing the ♢A and returning the suit, but he had wasted a lot of valuable mental energy.

West could have saved partner all that grief by continuing with the ♢J at trick two. Now East would know that it could not be wrong to overtake.

Quiz 8

Expect the Worst, Assume the Best

Good defenders make assumptions on every hand. Some assumptions, called inferences, are supported by evidence from the bidding or play. Other assumptions may have no basis in fact whatever, but the defenders must make them anyway because the alternative is to concede that the contract cannot be set.

Dlr: South
Vul: None

```
                    ♠ Q 9 7 6
                    ♡ K Q 5
                    ◇ A Q 10 7
                    ♣ 9 7
      ♠ 5                            ♠ A 8 3
      ♡ 10 4                         ♡ J 9 8 7 6
      ◇ 9 6 4 3 2        □          ◇ 5
      ♣ Q 10 5 3 2                   ♣ A K 8 6
                    ♠ K J 10 4 2
                    ♡ A 3 2
                    ◇ K J 8
                    ♣ J 4
```

WEST	NORTH	EAST	SOUTH
			1 ♠
Pass	3 ♠	Pass	4 ♠

West leads the ♣3. East wins the king and shifts to the singleton diamond. Upon winning the ♠A, he returns a *low* club to partner's queen and gets a diamond ruff for down one.

Obviously, East's play risks the loss of a trick. How does he know that partner has the ♣Q? He doesn't, but he can tell that the defenders' cause is hopeless otherwise. So he *assumes* that the cards lie so as to allow his defence to succeed.

A part of making assumptions is to count potential defensive tricks. (This helps you avoid making too many assumptions, or

assumptions that are inconsistent with the bidding or play.)
Counting your tricks is easier against a game or slam contract –
declarer will have most of the high cards, and your options may be
severely limited.

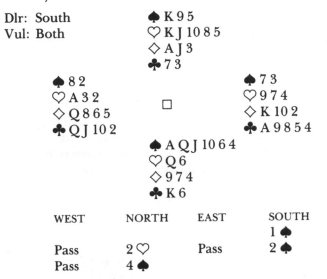

Dlr: South   ♠ K 9 5
Vul: Both   ♡ K J 10 8 5
                ◇ A J 3
                ♣ 7 3

♠ 8 2   ♠ 7 3
♡ A 3 2   ♡ 9 7 4
◇ Q 8 6 5   ◇ K 10 2
♣ Q J 10 2   ♣ A 9 8 5 4

                ♠ A Q J 10 6 4
                ♡ Q 6
                ◇ 9 7 4
                ♣ K 6

WEST	NORTH	EAST	SOUTH
			1 ♠
Pass	2 ♡	Pass	2 ♠
Pass	4 ♠		

West leads the ♣Q, and East wins the ace. East knows that the
hand is as good as over if declarer has solid trumps and the ♡A.
Each must 'give' West one major-suit trick, but it is too much to
expect him to have two. Therefore, East must hope that partner
holds the ◇Q, and it is essential to lead a diamond quickly. (An
'active' defence – see Quiz 9.)

The defenders often are obliged to make other assumptions
about declarer's hand.

Dlr: South   ♠ 7 6
Vul: Both   ♡ Q
                ◇ K J 4 3 2
                ♣ Q 10 9 5 4

♠ Q 9 4 3   ♠ 10 8 5
♡ 10 3   ♡ 8 6 2
◇ Q 9 8 7   ◇ 10 6 5
♣ K J 2   ♣ A 8 7 3

                ♠ A K J 2
                ♡ A K J 9 7 5 4
                ◇ A
                ♣ 6

WEST	NORTH	EAST	SOUTH
			2 ♣
Pass	3 ♦	Pass	3 ♡
Pass	4 ♣	Pass	4 ♡
Pass	5 ♡	Pass	5 ♠
Pass	6 ♡	All Pass	

West speculates with a club lead against South's 6♡. East wins the ace and shifts accurately to a trump. Declarer wins in dummy, ruffs a club, and runs all his trumps, putting West under a lot of pressure.

West can count seven tricks for declarer plus two side aces. It follows that if declarer has as many as two diamonds, the contract is cold – a diamond finesse will give an eleventh trick, and West is squeezed in the minors for the twelfth. So West has to assume that declarer holds the singleton ♦A. He must discard his diamonds and hang on to his spades.

Problems

1. Dlr: North
   Vul: Both

♠ A 8 3
♡ A 9 8
♦ K 8
♣ Q J 10 5 4

                    ♠ J 10 4 2
                    ♡ K 5
      □   ♦ J 9
                    ♣ A 9 8 7 6

WEST	NORTH	EAST	SOUTH
	1 ♣	Pass	1 ♡
Pass	1 NT	Pass	3 ♦
Pass	3 ♡	Pass	4 ♡
All Pass			

West, your partner, leads the ♣2. Plan your defence.

2. Dlr: South   ♠ A Q 10 4
        Vul: E-W   ♡ 5 4
                            ◇ 6 5 4
                            ♣ Q 7 4 3

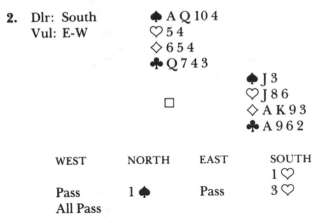

                                        ♠ J 3
                                        ♡ J 8 6
                            □   ◇ A K 9 3
                                        ♣ A 9 6 2

WEST	NORTH	EAST	SOUTH
			1 ♡
Pass	1 ♠	Pass	3 ♡
All Pass			

North must have seen you defend before – his pass of 3♡ was rather conservative. Anyway, West leads the ♣J. You judge to put up your ace when dummy ducks, and declarer drops the king. Plan your defence.

Solutions

1. The ♣A, a club ruff, and the ♡K will make up the defensive book. The setting trick must come from diamonds or spades, so you must assume that partner has either the ◇A or the ♠K. If he holds the ◇A, your play is immaterial – you either can give partner his club ruff right now or wait until you get in with the ♡K.

You therefore should assume that it's the ♠K partner holds. In that case, a spade return at trick two is vital. If you return a club instead, partner will be unable to lead a spade effectively from his side, and declarer will have time to draw trumps and discard spade losers on the clubs. The full deal:

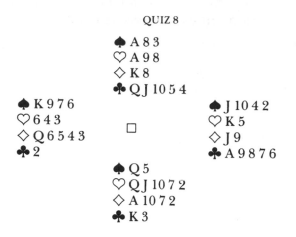

♠ A 8 3
♡ A 9 8
◇ K 8
♣ Q J 10 5 4

♠ K 9 7 6   ♠ J 10 4 2
♡ 6 4 3   ♡ K 5
◇ Q 6 5 4 3   □   ◇ J 9
♣ 2   ♣ A 9 8 7 6

♠ Q 5
♡ Q J 10 7 2
◇ A 10 7 2
♣ K 3

2. This will not be an easy contract to beat. There will be no spade tricks for the defence and no more in clubs. Partner can't be expected to provide two tricks in trumps, so you will have to look to diamonds for three tricks. At trick three, lead a *low* diamond, putting declarer to a guess if he has Q-10-x.

♠ A Q 10 4
♡ 5 4
◇ 6 5 4
♣ Q 7 4 3

♠ 9 8 7 2   ♠ J 3
♡ 10 9   ♡ J 8 6
◇ J 8 7   □   ◇ A K 9 3
♣ J 10 8 5   ♣ A 9 6 2

♠ K 6 5
♡ A K Q 7 3 2
◇ Q 10 2
♣ K

Assuming declarer misguesses, as most would, partner will win the ◇J and return the suit for you to cash two more winners. Then the lead of the thirteenth diamond will promote the setting trick in trumps.

Problems

3. Dlr: South ♠ Q 5
  Vul: N-S ♡ 10 9 8 4 3
     ◇ K Q 3
     ♣ A J 2

♠ 10 8 4 2
♡ A Q 2
◇ 10 7 4 □
♣ K 10 9

WEST	NORTH	EAST	SOUTH
			1 ◇
Pass	1 ♡	Pass	1 NT
Pass	3 NT	All Pass	

You, West, lead the ♠2. Partner produces the ace and returns the three. Declarer plays the jack from hand and dummy's queen wins the trick. Declarer now leads a heart to his jack. Plan your defence.

4. Dlr: West ♠ K Q 6 3
  Vul: N-S ♡ J 3
     ◇ A Q 10 8
     ♣ K Q 4

        ♠ A 10 4
        ♡ 9 4
    □   ◇ 7 6 5 3 2
        ♣ A J 2

WEST	NORTH	EAST	SOUTH
Pass	1 NT	Pass	4 ♡
All Pass			

West, your partner, leads the ♠2 against the heart game. You capture dummy's king with the ace. What do you return?

Solutions

3.
        ♠ Q 5
        ♡ 10 9 8 4 3
        ◇ K Q 3
        ♣ A J 2

♠ 10 8 4 2   ♠ A 9 6 3
♡ A Q 2   □   ♡ 7 6 5
◇ 10 7 4   ◇ 8 6 5
♣ K 10 9   ♣ Q 4 3

        ♠ K J 7
        ♡ K J
        ◇ A J 9 2
        ♣ 8 7 6 5

At the table, West won the ♡Q and knocked out declarer's last spade stopper. Declarer gave up a further trick to the ♡A. West cashed his good spade. Declarer claimed the rest, making nine tricks.

South had to have the ♡K for his opening bid, so at least nine offensive tricks were in view. Clearly, West should have shifted to the ♣10 at trick four, since a spade continuation could set up only four tricks for the defence. If declarer ducked the first club, either another club lead or a switch back to spades would establish the setting trick.

4.
        ♠ K Q 6 3
        ♡ J 3
        ◇ A Q 10 8
        ♣ K Q 4

♠ J 9 5 2   ♠ A 10 4
♡ K 8 5   □   ♡ 9 4
◇ J 9   ◇ 7 6 5 3 2
♣ 10 8 6 5   ♣ A J 2

        ♠ 8 7
        ♡ A Q 10 7 6 2
        ◇ K 4
        ♣ 9 7 3

Partner must have at least one trump trick to give the defence a chance. Even so, two club tricks probably will be needed. Return a low club, playing West for the ♣10 and declarer for three or more clubs.

The alternative is to try a diamond, playing declarer for

However, partner would not have led a *low* spade (suggesting interest in no other suit) if he had a diamond void.

Quiz 9

Get Active or Go Passive?

Most defences against a suit contract boil down to one of two approaches. In one scenario, declarer has ample trick-taking power: lots of high cards, a good side suit in dummy, or perhaps a big trump fit combined with ruffing power. He is destined to make his contract *unless the defence can acquire the setting trick first*. In an *active* defence, therefore, the defenders are anxious to cash everything in sight, and they are willing to take chances to set up whatever tricks they need quickly.

In contrast, a passive defence is best when declarer has limited values and will have to dig hard for his tricks. In this case, the defence wants to *avoid* cashing winners, leading away from honours and breaking new suits. Getting too busy on defence can only help declarer avoid some of his potential losers – *losers that he is destined to lose in any case*.

Look at these two hands:

```
Dlr: South        ♠ J 9
Vul: Both         ♡ A 10 4
                  ◇ A J 4
                  ♣ K Q 10 9 4
   ♠ 10 5 4 3                    ♠ A K Q 7 6
   ♡ 8 5             □           ♡ K 2
   ◇ Q 9 5 2                     ◇ K 8 6
   ♣ J 7 2                       ♣ 8 5 3
                  ♠ 8 2
                  ♡ Q J 9 7 6 3
                  ◇ 10 7 3
                  ♣ A 6
```

South opened 2♡ (weak), and North jumped to 4♡. West led a spade, and East cashed the queen and king. At trick three, East shifted to a diamond away from his king, and West's queen

75

forced dummy's ace. When declarer lost the trump finesse, East
was able to cash the ♢K for down one.

This was an effective *active* defence. East could see that declarer
would be able to take ten tricks eventually with heart and club
winners, so it was necessary to take a chance in diamonds.

Dlr: South   ♠ A K 5 4
Vul: N-S   ♡ 10 6 5
                    ♢ K 7 6
                    ♣ 7 5 4

♠ Q J 10 6   ♠ 9 8 7 3
♡ J 4 3   □   ♡ 9 8
♢ Q 10 5   ♢ A 9 8 4
♣ J 9 6   ♣ K 8 3

                    ♠ 2
                    ♡ A K Q 7 2
                    ♢ J 3 2
                    ♣ A Q 10 2

WEST	NORTH	EAST	SOUTH
			1 ♡
Pass	1 ♠	Pass	2 ♣
Pass	3 ♡	Pass	4 ♡
All Pass			

West leads the ♠Q. Declarer takes the top spades, discarding a
diamond, and plays a club to the ten and jack. Here, West must
exit *safely* with a spade, which gives declarer nothing that isn't his
anyhow.

The lead of either minor suit will cost a trick directly, while a
trump exit gives declarer a dummy entry to take another club
finesse.

Typically, trump leads by the defenders are a good way to get
out of the lead without giving anything away. Of course, trump
leads also may reduce declarer's trick-taking power.

Dlr: South   ♠ 8
Vul: None   ♡ K 6 5 2
              ◇ Q 8 7
              ♣ J 8 5 4 2

♠ K 5   ♠ Q 10 7 6 2
♡ Q 10 8 7   ☐   ♡ J 9
◇ 9 6 4   ◇ A 3 2
♣ A K 10 6   ♣ Q 9 7

              ♠ A J 9 4 3
              ♡ A 4 3
              ◇ K J 10 5
              ♣ 3

South ends in 2◇, having opened 1♠. West lays down a high club on opening lead. After seeing dummy he definitely should switch to trumps. With dummy so weak in high cards, declarer will be seeking spade ruffs.

A more spectacular example:

Dlr: East   ♠ 5
Vul: Both   ♡ J 4
              ◇ Q J 6 5 3
              ♣ 10 8 6 5 3

♠ J 9 3   ♠ K 10 8 7
♡ A Q   ☐   ♡ 7 5 2
◇ 10 9 7 2   ◇ K 8 4
♣ J 9 7 2   ♣ A K Q

              ♠ A Q 6 4 2
              ♡ K 10 9 8 6 3
              ◇ A
              ♣ 4

WEST	NORTH	EAST	SOUTH
		1 NT	2 ♡
2 NT	Pass	Pass	3 ♠
Pass	4 ♡	Pass	Pass
Dbl	All Pass		

After West led the ◇10, declarer almost made his unlikely contract. The play went: ◇A, ♠A, spade ruff, ◇Q covered and ruffed, spade ruff, ◇J for a club discard, club ruff. With K-10-9-8 of trumps left, South was sure of two more tricks, and he conceded only 200 points despite his risky bidding.

A club lead and trump switch would make the penalty 800, but that requires a crystal ball. The technically correct lead, which results in down two, is the ♡A. West knows that his side has general strength and, since North took a heart preference, there is a danger that South will ruff some spades in dummy. On a trump lead and continuation, West loses a trump trick but gains two tricks in return.

It is strange that on some other hands, the defenders' strategy may be to *force* dummy to ruff. For example:

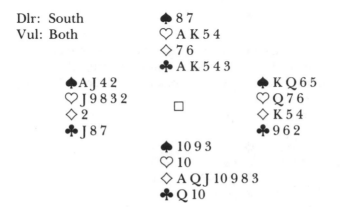

Dlr: South
Vul: Both

♠ 8 7
♡ A K 5 4
◇ 7 6
♣ A K 5 4 3

♠ A J 4 2
♡ J 9 8 3 2
◇ 2
♣ J 8 7

□

♠ K Q 6 5
♡ Q 7 6
◇ K 5 4
♣ 9 6 2

♠ 10 9 3
♡ 10
◇ A Q J 10 9 8 3
♣ Q 10

South plays in 5◇ after opening with a 3◇ pre-empt. West leads the ♠A and continues with the two to East's queen. Declarer is marked with another spade, so clearly East should continue with a third spade, forcing dummy. Declarer can no longer pick up the ◇K.

There are, of course, plenty of other times when forcing dummy is the right defence. We'll see some of them in this Quiz and later on. Also, in Quiz 11, we will examine other defensive strategies – specifically, those that surround play in the trump suit.

Problems

1. Dlr: South   ♠ A J 4
    Vul: Both   ♡ 8 5 2
                    ◇ K 4
                    ♣ A K J 10 5

                                        ♠ 8 6
                                        ♡ Q 7 3
                          ☐   ◇ A 9 6 2
                                        ♣ 8 7 6 4

WEST	NORTH	EAST	SOUTH
			1 ♠
Pass	3 ♣	Pass	3 ♠
Pass	4 ♠	All Pass	

West, your partner, leads the ◇J. Plan your defence.

2. Dlr: South   ♠ 8 7 5 3
    Vul: N-S   ♡ K Q 3
                    ◇ Q 10 3
                    ♣ 8 7 2

    ♠ K Q 10 6
    ♡ 7 6
    ◇ 9 8 6   ☐
    ♣ A K 10 3

WEST	NORTH	EAST	SOUTH
			1 ♡
Dbl	2 ♡	Pass	3 ◇
Pass	4 ♡	All Pass	

You, West, lead the ♣A – two, four, five. At trick two, you switch to the ♠K. This time East encourages with the nine, and declarer follows low. What do you lead to trick three?

Solutions

1. The situation is desperate. Declarer has only one loser in diamonds and none at all in the black suits, so the heart must be very kind to the defence. Furthermore, you must grab what

heart tricks you can right now, before declarer draws trumps and throws his heart losers on the clubs.

West holding the ace and king, would have led a heart, but he could have A-J-10. You must assume that is the case. Whether declarer plays the ◇K from dummy or not, win the ◇A and lead the ♡Q.

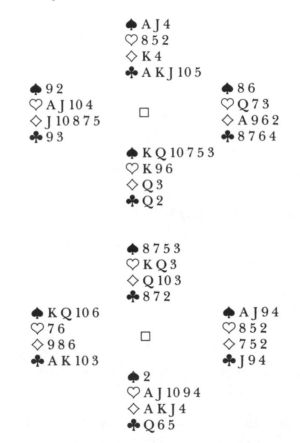

              ♠ A J 4
              ♡ 8 5 2
              ◇ K 4
              ♣ A K J 10 5

♠ 9 2   ♠ 8 6
♡ A J 10 4   ♡ Q 7 3
◇ J 10 8 7 5   □   ◇ A 9 6 2
♣ 9 3   ♣ 8 7 6 4

              ♠ K Q 10 7 5 3
              ♡ K 9 6
              ◇ Q 3
              ♣ Q 2

2.   ♠ 8 7 5 3
              ♡ K Q 3
              ◇ Q 10 3
              ♣ 8 7 2

♠ K Q 10 6   ♠ A J 9 4
♡ 7 6   ♡ 8 5 2
◇ 9 8 6   □   ◇ 7 5 2
♣ A K 10 3   ♣ J 9 4

              ♠ 2
              ♡ A J 10 9 4
              ◇ A K J 4
              ♣ Q 6 5

This is a deceptively difficult problem. The appearance of the dummy suggests a passive defence, and a spade continuation, forcing declarer to ruff, seems safe enough. But in fact it will help declarer to reverse the dummy. The play will go: second round of spades, ruffed; ♡A; heart to the queen; spade ruff; diamond to the ten; spade ruff; diamond to the queen; ♡K, drawing the last trump; diamond to the king; ◇A. That's ten tricks.

The *super*passive exit of a trump at trick three will ruin declarer's timing for the dummy reversal and defeat the hand.

Problems

3. Dlr: South
Vul: None

> ♠ 6 5
> ♡ J 10
> ◇ A J 6 5 4
> ♣ 7 6 5 4

♠ K Q 10 3
♡ Q 9 2
◇ 7 3 2
♣ K 10 8

☐

WEST	NORTH	EAST	SOUTH
			1 ♡
Pass	1 NT	Pass	2 ♠
Pass	3 ◇	Pass	3 ♡
Pass	4 ♡	All Pass	

You, West, elect to lead the ♠K. Partner plays the nine and declarer plays small. What do you lead next?

4. Dlr: East
Vul: Both

> ♠ 7 6
> ♡ Q 10 7 4
> ◇ 7 5
> ♣ K 8 7 6 5

☐

♠ K 9 3
♡ A J 9 6 3
◇ A 8
♣ J 9 4

WEST	NORTH	EAST	SOUTH
		1 ♡	Dbl
2 ♡	Pass	Pass	Dbl
Pass	3 ♣	Pass	3 ◇
All Pass			

West, your partner, leads the ♡2. Dummy plays low, and your nine holds the first trick, declarer following with the eight. Plan your defence.

Solutions

3. East's signal indicates a spade honour, probably the jack. Declarer therefore has some spade losers, and he surely will want to ruff them. Dummy is weak in high cards, and the diamond suit is unlikely to run – on the bidding, declarer won't have much help in diamonds.

A trump shift is indicated, but care must be taken. The full deal:

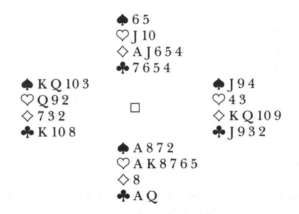

       ♠ 6 5
       ♡ J 10
       ◇ A J 6 5 4
       ♣ 7 6 5 4

♠ K Q 10 3   ♠ J 9 4
♡ Q 9 2   ♡ 4 3
◇ 7 3 2   □   ◇ K Q 10 9
♣ K 10 8   ♣ J 9 3 2

       ♠ A 8 7 2
       ♡ A K 8 7 6 5
       ◇ 8
       ♣ A Q

A low trump switch still will give declarer a cakewalk – he will take six trump tricks in hand, one spade ruff, and three side aces. Try switching to the ♡Q, smothering two of declarer's honours at once. Now declarer gains nothing by ruffing a spade because your nine of trumps is promoted.

Double-dummy, declarer still could make the contract by declining the club finesse, stripping you of your diamonds, and throwing you in with a major suit to lead a club into his tenace.

4. You are in a dilemma. Declarer surely has three or four spades, so you would like to switch to trumps to stop a ruff. However, there is a danger that declarer also has club length. If you release control of the trump suit by playing ace and another, declarer may establish clubs for all the tricks he needs.

The full deal:

```
                    ♠ 7 6
                    ♡ Q 10 7 4
                    ◇ 7 5
                    ♣ K 8 7 6 5
  ♠ Q 10 8 5 4                      ♠ K 9 3
  ♡ K 5 2                           ♡ A J 9 6 3
  ◇ 9 4 2            □              ◇ A 8
  ♣ Q 10                           ♣ J 9 4
                    ♠ A J 2
                    ♡ 8
                    ◇ K Q J 10 6 3
                    ♣ A 3 2
```

The winning defence is not easy to spot. East must switch to the ◇8 at trick two.

If declarer concedes a spade, East wins, cashes the ◇A, and leads a spade. The defence can cash a spade when they win a club trick. Nor does it help declarer to duck a club immediately – he'll run into a club ruff.

Quiz 10

Killing Declarer's Suit

In Quiz 9, we contrasted an *active* approach (the defence is obliged to seek fast tricks) with a *passive* approach (the defenders need only sit back and wait for tricks that are bound to fall into their laps sooner or later). In general, the right approach is determined by how much trick-taking power dummy has: if there are only a few scattered high cards, no ruffing power, and no good suit, go passive; if there are plenty of tricks, get active. (For still more on this important concept, see Quizzes 8, 13, and 20.)

One other approach must be considered. This one is based on the idea that if the defenders can deny declarer his best source of tricks, the contract is likely to fail. Here is an illustration.

Dlr: South
Vul: None

	♠ 8 5	
	♡ 7 6	
	♢ Q 10 8	
	♣ A K 7 6 5 4	

♠ J 9 6 2		♠ A K Q 7
♡ Q 10 5 4	□	♡ K J 9 3 2
♢ 4 3 2		♢ 5
♣ 10 9		♣ Q 8 3

	♠ 10 4 3	
	♡ A 8	
	♢ A K J 9 7 6	
	♣ J 2	

WEST	NORTH	EAST	SOUTH
			1 ♢
Pass	2 ♣	Dbl	2 ♢
Pass	3 ♢	Pass	3 ♡
Pass	5 ♢	All Pass	

84

West leads the ♠2, and ninety-nine out of one hundred East defenders would take two top spades and shift to a heart. Declarer wins the ace, cashes a high trump, establishes clubs with a ruff, draws two more rounds of trumps ending in dummy, and takes a heart discard on a good club, making five.

At trick three, East should reason that declarer surely has the ♡A, so E-W have no fast heart tricks to take. The key to the defence is keeping declarer from using dummy's clubs. West's opening lead marks declarer with a third spade, so East continues with the ♠A, forcing dummy to ruff. Declarer's late entry to the club suit vanishes, and he has no way to dispose of his heart loser.

Killing declarer's suit is a very common type of defence against a no-trump contract. The most spectacular example is the well-known Merrimac Coup (illustrated elsewhere). Here is another common situation, similar to one shown in Quiz 6.

```
Dlr: South          ♠ A 6 2
Vul: N-S            ♡ 6 5 4
                    ◇ K J 10 9 5
                    ♣ 7 6
    ♠ Q 10 8 4                      ♠ 9 7 5
    ♡ J 9 8 2                       ♡ Q 10
    ◇ 8 4 2          □              ◇ A Q 6
    ♣ Q 3                           ♣ J 10 9 8 5
                    ♠ K J 3
                    ♡ A K 7 3
                    ◇ 7 3
                    ♣ A K 4 2
```

South plays in 3NT, having shown a strong, balanced hand. West leads the ♠4, which goes to declarer's jack. Declarer now plays a diamond to dummy's ten. If East wins this trick, the defence is finished: declarer wins the spade return with the king, plays his other diamond to dislodge East's ace, and takes three diamonds, three spades, and the two side suit ace-kings for an overtrick.

East can beat the contract by allowing dummy to win the first diamond. Declarer now has lost the timing to bring in the diamond suit, and barring an obscure throw-in, he must settle for eight tricks.

Problems

1. Dlr: North   ♠ A K J
   Vul: Both   ♡ A K 5 4 3
                  ◇ K 4 3
                  ♣ 6 2

   ♠ Q 10 4 3
   ♡ J 2   □
   ◇ Q 10 8 5
   ♣ K 4 3

WEST	NORTH	EAST	SOUTH
	1 ♡	Pass	1 NT
Pass	2 NT	Pass	3 NT
All Pass			

You, West, lead the ♠3. Dummy's jack wins, dampening your hopes somewhat. At trick two, declarer leads the ♣2 – five, ten. How do you defend?

2. Dlr: South   ♠ K
   Vul: Both   ♡ 9 7 6 3
                  ◇ J 8 2
                  ♣ K 10 8 6 3
                                    ♠ 5 2
                                    ♡ Q 10 8
                        □   ◇ A 9 4
                                    ♣ A J 9 5 4

WEST	NORTH	EAST	SOUTH
			1 ♠
Pass	1 NT	Pass	4 ♠
All Pass			

West, your partner, starts the ◇5 against South's game. You win the ace and declarer drops the queen. What is your next play?

Solutions

1.

```
          ♠ A K J
          ♡ A K 5 4 3
          ◇ K 1 3
          ♣ 6 2
♠ Q 10 4 3              ♠ 9 6 5
♡ J 2                  ♡ Q 10 9 7 6
◇ Q 10 8 5    □        ◇ 9 7 6
♣ K 4 3                ♣ A 5
          ♠ 8 7 2
          ♡ 8
          ◇ A J 2
          ♣ Q J 10 9 8 7
```

You should allow the ♣10 to hold. On the deal above, if you take the ♣K, declarer has time to establish clubs and will end up making two overtricks. This defence also would be necessary on other layouts – for instance, declarer could have long clubs headed by the A-Q-10 or A-J-10.

If your clubs were K-x, it still would be correct to duck the first round.

2.

```
          ♠ K
          ♡ 9 7 6 3
          ◇ J 8 2
          ♣ K 10 8 6 3
♠ 8 4 3                ♠ 5 2
♡ K 5 4                ♡ Q 10 8
◇ 10 7 6 5 3  □        ◇ A 9 4
♣ Q 7                  ♣ A J 9 5 4
          ♠ A Q J 10 9 7 6
          ♡ A J 2
          ◇ K Q
          ♣ 2
```

Partner has at most five diamonds, so declarer has another diamond, probably the king. Since a discard may be coming up on the ◇J, switch to a trump, removing declarer's only entry to dummy. Your heart and club tricks can wait.

Playing ace and another club, trying to give partner a ruff, is a weak defence. If partner had a singleton club, he would have led it.

Problems

3. Dlr: South   ♠ A K 6 5 4
      Vul: None   ♡ Q 9 3
                   ◇ A K J
                   ♣ J 3

                               ♠ J 8 2
                               ♡ K J 10 7 2
                 □   ◇ Q 10 8
                               ♣ A 2

WEST	NORTH	EAST	SOUTH
			3 ♣
Pass	3 ♠	Pass	3 NT
All Pass			

Partner delights you by leading the ♡8. You place your ten on dummy's nine, and declarer plays the four. What do you lead at trick two?

4. Dlr: South   ♠ A K 6 4
      Vul: Both   ♡ 6 5
                   ◇ A J 4 3 2
                   ♣ J 8

   ♠ J 7 2
   ♡ K Q 10 9 3
   ◇ K 10 8   □
   ♣ A 4

WEST	NORTH	EAST	SOUTH
			1 ♣
1 ♡	2 ◇	Pass	3 ♣
Pass	3 ♠	Pass	3 NT
All Pass			

You, West, lead the ♡Q, which in your methods asks partner to drop the jack if he has it. The play to the first trick goes queen, five, two, seven. How do you continue?

Solutions

3.

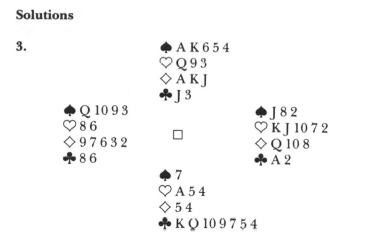

```
                    ♠ A K 6 5 4
                    ♡ Q 9 3
                    ◇ A K J
                    ♣ J 3
♠ Q 10 9 3                          ♠ J 8 2
♡ 8 6                               ♡ K J 10 7 2
◇ 9 7 6 3 2         □               ◇ Q 10 8
♣ 8 6                               ♣ A 2
                    ♠ 7
                    ♡ A 5 4
                    ◇ 5 4
                    ♣ K Q 10 9 7 5 4
```

Return the ♡K to knock out declarer's ace. This should be the only entry to his club suit; with seven good clubs, the ♡A, and the ♠Q, he would be too strong to pre-empt at this vulnerability. Later you will hold up the ♣A once, and declarer's hand will take no further part in the play.

The sacrifice of a high card to dislodge declarer's entry is called a Merrimac Coup. During the Spanish-American War, a ship of the same name was deliberately sunk by the Americans in the middle of a Cuban harbour channel. The intent was to neutralize the Spanish ships in port.

4.

```
                    ♠ A K 6 4
                    ♡ 6 5
                    ◇ A J 4 3 2
                    ♣ J 8
♠ J 7 2                             ♠ Q 10 9 8
♡ K Q 10 9 3        □               ♡ 8 4 2
◇ K 10 8                            ◇ 9 7 6
♣ A 4                              ♣ 7 5 3
                    ♠ 5 3
                    ♡ A J 7
                    ◇ Q 5
                    ♣ K Q 10 9 6 2
```

Lead the ♡10. Declarer may be gratified with his 'Bath Coup' until he realizes that the only sure entry to his club suit is gone.

As in the previous problem, you will win the second club.

Then a spade switch will limit declarer to four diamonds, one heart, one club, and two spades. (If declarer cashes his second heart winner early, he sets up five defensive tricks for you.)

Quiz 11

Around the Trump Suit

There will be an extended introduction in this section, since many interesting defensive techniques revolve round the trump suit. Our discussion will touch upon the forcing defence, trump control, ruff-and-discards, trump promotions, and the upper-cut. These are all areas in which the defenders can create unexpected tricks.

Every player enjoys taking ruffing tricks with small trumps. (See Quiz 1 for more about seeking ruffs.) However, when the defenders find themselves with certain combinations of *high* trumps, ruffing still may gain.

<pre>
                753
A J 10   □   K 6
                Q9842
</pre>

East ruffs with the king, and West's trumps are normally worth three more tricks.

<pre>
                42
A K J 8   □   Q
                1097653
</pre>

East ruffs with the queen, and the defence may take five trump tricks instead of four.

<pre>
                Q652
A   □   J 109
                K8743
</pre>

If declarer leads towards the queen, E-W will take only one trick. But if West gets a ruff with the ace, East's holding is promoted.

There is a natural psychological barrier to winning trump

tricks in defence. Defenders tend to regard the trump suit as declarer's inviolable domain. Many players, for example, would miss the following easy defence, which bears some relation to the positions mentioned above.

Dlr: North   ♠ 6 4
Vul: N-S   ♡ Q 6 4
                    ◇ K 6 5 4
                    ♣ A K J 3

♠ K 9 2   ♠ 8 5
♡ 9 2   ♡ A K J 10 5 3
◇ 9 8 7 3   □   ◇ A 10 2
♣ 10 9 8 7   ♣ 4 2

                    ♠ A Q J 10 7 3
                    ♡ 8 7
                    ◇ Q J
                    ♣ Q 6 5

WEST	NORTH	EAST	SOUTH
	1 ♣	1 ♡	1 ♠
Pass	1 NT	Pass	3 ♠
All Pass			

West leads a heart. On the third round, declarer ruffs with the queen, and West must *discard*. If he overruffs with the king, he gains nothing – it is as though declarer had lost a finesse to the king, which is what would happen anyway. Overruffing with a natural trump winner is seldom right.

Declarer goes to dummy with a club and plays a spade to the jack and king. Now West puts partner in with the ◇A, and a fourth heart is led. Whether declarer ruffs low or high, West is bound to score the ♠9.

This play, called a *trump promotion*, has a first cousin, the *uppercut*.

Dlr: South   ♠ Q 7 4
Vul: None   ♡ K Q 9 6
                 ◇ K Q 3
                 ♣ 9 6 4

♠ J 8 3		♠ 10
♡ A 5	□	♡ J 10 8 7 4 3
◇ 10 4		◇ 8 7 5 2
♣ A K J 8 7 2		♣ 5 3

                 ♠ A K 9 6 5 2
                 ♡ 2
                 ◇ A J 9 6
                 ♣ Q 10

WEST	NORTH	EAST	SOUTH
			1 ♠
2 ♣	Dbl[1]	Pass	2 ♠
Pass	4 ♠	All Pass	

[1] negative

West cashes two top clubs and the ♡A. There are no more side-suit tricks for the defence, so West tries for the setting trick in trumps by leading a *low* club at trick four. East is obliged to ruff with his trump ten, and declarer, forced to spend an honour to overruff, must lose a trump trick to West.

Note that cashing the ♡A was essential. If West led a club at trick three, declarer could discard his losing heart instead of overruffing. In all the situations seen so far, the defenders *must* cash all their side-suit winners before trying to promote trump tricks; otherwise, declarer may be able to counter with a loser-on-loser play.

In a *forcing game*, the defenders make declarer ruff so many times that he uses up all his trumps. Even if they don't establish some small trumps, the defenders may gain control of the play so they can cash winners elsewhere.

Dlr: North
Vul: None

♠ A K
♡ J 9 4
♢ Q 10 8 5
♣ A Q J 5

♠ 10 8 5 4 2
♡ 5
♢ A 7 4 3
♣ 9 7 3

□

♠ 9 7
♡ A 8 7 2
♢ K 9 6 2
♣ K 10 4

♠ Q J 6 3
♡ K Q 10 6 3
♢ J
♣ 8 6 2

WEST	NORTH	EAST	SOUTH
	1 NT	Pass	2 ♣
Pass	2 ♢	Pass	2 ♡
Pass	3 ♣	Pass	4 ♡
All Pass			

South's sequence was game-invitational and suggested length in both majors. North's 3♣ bid was an intelligent effort to pinpoint his values.

West led a low club, finessed to the king. East, with four trumps, hoped to force declarer in diamonds. (A diamond lead could not cost even if declarer had A-x, since declarer could throw his losing diamond on a club anyway.) East was careful to lead the ♢K first, an essential play. Declarer ruffed the diamond continuation and led trumps. East won the second round and played yet another diamond. Declarer now had either to give West the ♢A or to lose control and concede a trick to East's long trump.

In many forcing games, a defender must wait to force declarer until only one of the opposing hands has some trumps.

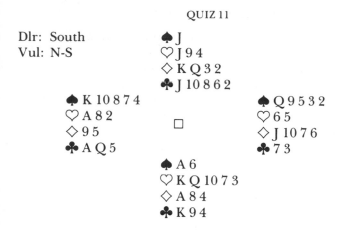

Dlr: South
Vul: N-S

♠ J
♡ J 9 4
◇ K Q 3 2
♣ J 10 8 6 2

♠ K 10 8 7 4
♡ A 8 2
◇ 9 5
♣ A Q 5

□

♠ Q 9 5 3 2
♡ 6 5
◇ J 10 7 6
♣ 7 3

♠ A 6
♡ K Q 10 7 3
◇ A 8 4
♣ K 9 4

South played in 4♡, and West led a spade. Declarer won, ruffed a spade, and led the ♡J. West *ducked* – had he won, he couldn't have made an effective return. However, when declarer led a second trump, West won and continued spades. Declarer ruffed in hand, drew the last trump (leaving himself with one), went to dummy with a diamond, and led the ♣J. West won the queen and forced out declarer's last trump with another spade lead. He later got in with the ♣A and cashed a spade for down one.

Control of the trump suit can be just as important to the defenders as to declarer. For example, on many hands a defender must not release the trump ace until the proper time.

Dlr: South
Vul: Both

♠ J 5
♡ 8 5 3
◇ A 6 5 4
♣ J 7 6 5

♠ Q 10 7 4 3
♡ A 6 2
◇ K J 10
♣ Q 3

□

♠ 9 8
♡ 9 7
◇ Q 9 7 3
♣ K 10 9 8 4

♠ A K 6 2
♡ K Q J 10 4
◇ 8 2
♣ A 2

N-S reach an aggressive heart game. West leads a spade, won by dummy's jack. Declarer leads a heart to his king. If West wins this and plays another spade, declarer wins, draws one more trump, and safely ruffs his spade loser in dummy.

West does better to duck the first round of trumps. Declarer can't ruff his fourth spade at this point, since East can overruff; but if declarer plays a second round of trumps, West can win and lead a third round, stranding declarer with a spade loser.

Beginners are taught that giving declarer a ruff-and-discard is the unpardonable sin. Nevertheless, if declarer hasn't any losers left, a ruff-and-discard can't cost anything, and it may be an effective way of weakening declarer's trump holding. More often, it can merely be a safe way to exit.

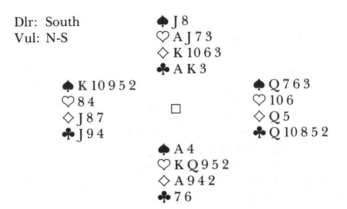

Dlr: South
Vul: N-S

♠ J 8
♡ A J 7 3
◇ K 10 6 3
♣ A K 3

♠ K 10 9 5 2
♡ 8 4
◇ J 8 7
♣ J 9 4

♠ Q 7 6 3
♡ 10 6
◇ Q 5
♣ Q 10 8 5 2

♠ A 4
♡ K Q 9 5 2
◇ A 9 4 2
♣ 7 6

In a matchpoint event, South played in the normal contract of 4♡. West led the ♠10 – jack, queen, ace. Declarer drew trumps, eliminated clubs, and exited with a spade. West knew that declarer had five hearts and two clubs. If a spade continuation gave him a ruff-and-discard, then he had four diamonds, and he would only be throwing away a winner. So West led a third spade, and declarer had to lose another trick.

Problems

1. Dlr: South
    Vul: N-S

♠ K J 4
♡ K Q 3 2
◇ J 6 3
♣ 9 5 3

♠ Q 5
♡ 8 5 4
◇ A 10 7 2
♣ K Q 10 4

WEST	NORTH	EAST	SOUTH
			1 NT
Pass	2 ♣	Pass	2 ♠
Pass	3 NT	Pass	4 ♡
All Pass			

You, West, lead the ♣K – three, eight, two. The ♣4 goes to partner's jack and declarer's ace. Declarer draws three rounds of trumps, partner discarding the ◇5. A spade to the jack wins, partner playing the ten. Declarer cashes the ♠K and ♠A. East following with the seven and eight while you discard a diamond. Declarer now exits with a club to you. East following. How do you defend?

2. Dlr: South
Vul: N-S

          ♠ J 10 4
          ♡ K 6 3
          ◇ Q J 10
          ♣ A J 10 3

                        ♠ K 8 7
          □   ♡ A Q 10 8 7
                        ◇ K 3 2
                        ♣ 8 7

WEST	NORTH	EAST	SOUTH
			1 ♠
Pass	2 ♣	2 ♡	Pass
Pass	2 ♠	Pass	4 ♠
All Pass			

West, your partner, leads the ♡J, which wins. Another heart is led, and you win the queen and ace, partner discarding a low club. How do you continue?

Solutions

1. Lead the thirteenth club. True, you are giving declarer the dreaded ruff-and-discard, but he has a losing spade to ruff, so he is going to make his two remaining trumps separately anyway. What you must avoid is breaking the diamond suit.

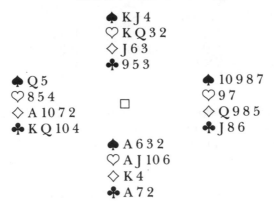

♠ K J 4
♡ K Q 3 2
♢ J 6 3
♣ 9 5 3

♠ Q 5
♡ 8 5 4
♢ A 10 7 2
♣ K Q 10 4

♠ 10 9 8 7
♡ 9 7
♢ Q 9 8 5
♣ J 8 6

♠ A 6 3 2
♡ A J 10 6
♢ K 4
♣ A 7 2

2. Lead a fourth round of hearts. Declarer is marked with the ♢A and a club honour on the bidding. Since he has no more side-suit losers, a ruff-and-discard won't help him.

How can it help your side? The full deal:

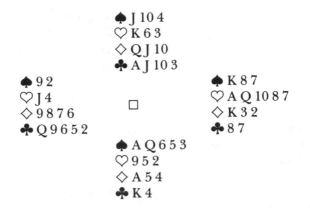

♠ J 10 4
♡ K 6 3
♢ Q J 10
♣ A J 10 3

♠ 9 2
♡ J 4
♢ 9 8 7 6
♣ Q 9 6 5 2

♠ K 8 7
♡ A Q 10 8 7
♢ K 3 2
♣ 8 7

♠ A Q 6 5 3
♡ 9 5 2
♢ A 5 4
♣ K 4

West ruffs with the ♠9, forcing a trump honour from dummy, and your trump holding provides the setting trick.

Problems

3. Dlr: North   ♠ A K Q 4
     Vul: N-S   ♡ J 8 5 3
                        ◇ Q 10 5 3
                        ♣ Q

   ♠ 5 3
   ♡ K Q 10 9 2   ☐
   ◇ A 9 4
   ♣ 8 7 6

WEST	NORTH	EAST	SOUTH
	1 ◇	Pass	2 ♣
Pass	2 NT	Pass	3 ♠
Pass	4 ♠	All Pass	

You, West, lead the ♡K. Partner overtakes with the ace and returns a heart to your queen. What now?

4. Dlr: South   ♠ K 8
     Vul: Both   ♡ J 6
                        ◇ A K J 8 7
                        ♣ Q J 5 3

   ♠ 6 3
   ♡ K Q 10 7 5 4 3   ☐
   ◇ Q 9 3
   ♣ 10

WEST	NORTH	EAST	SOUTH
			1 ♣
3 ♡	4 ◇	Pass	4 ♠
Pass	5 ♣	All Pass	

You, West, lead the ♡K. Partner overtakes with the ace and returns a heart to your king. Wht do you play at trick three?

Solutions

3. Cash the ◇A and play a third heart. Once East shows the ♡A, declarer needs the ♣AK and ◇K to have anything close to a hand worth a game force. Your only chance is to find partner with the ♠J.

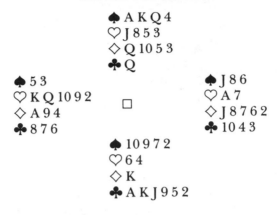

Note the need to take the ♢A before you try for the trump promotion.

4.   Lead another heart. The trump suit is your only hope for the setting trick.

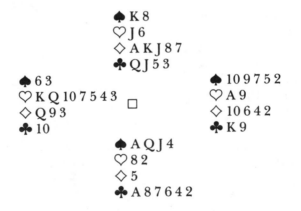

As it happens, today is your lucky day. If declarer ruffs low in dummy, East overruffs with the nine, forcing declarer's ace. If dummy ruffs with an honour, East will discard, of course.

Quiz 12

To Ruff or Not to Ruff?

Edmond Hoyle was an eighteenth-century expert on whist. Even today, his name is used to invoke learned authority over all sorts of card games. A lot of people probably think there is somebody named Hoyle alive and holding court in Las Vegas.

One of this gentleman's dicta at whist was 'When in doubt, win the trick'. But card-play technique has progressed in the past few hundred years, and such blanket pieces of advice no longer enjoy unquestioned acceptance.

In Quiz 11, we saw that refusing to overruff can be a necessary ingredient in a trump promotion. Here are a couple of additional positions:

$$\begin{array}{ccc} & \text{A 5} & \\ \text{J 8 3 2} & \square & \text{Q} \\ & \text{K 10 9 7 6 4} & \end{array}$$

This suit is trumps, and East leads a side suit in which West and declarer are void. If declarer ruffs with the ten, West must discard to wind up with two tricks.

$$\begin{array}{ccc} & \text{Q 4} & \\ \text{7 5} & \square & \text{K J 9} \\ & \text{A 10 8 6 3 2} & \end{array}$$

West leads a side suit in which East and dummy are void. If dummy ruffs with the queen, East must discard.

There are quite a few other situations where a defender may decline to take the short view by ruffing or overruffing. If his calculations are correct, the easy trick he is passing up will come back with interest.

Dlr: North   ♠ K 5
Vul: N-S   ♡ J 6 3
Matchpoints   ◇ 7 6 3
                    ♣ K Q 7 6 3

♠ Q J 10 8   ♠ 7 3
♡ 10 5 4   □   ♡ K Q 8 7
◇ K J 10 8 5 2   ◇ Q 9 4
♣ −   ♣ 10 9 8 4

                    ♠ A 9 6 4 2
                    ♡ A 9 2
                    ◇ A
                    ♣ A J 5 2

WEST	NORTH	EAST	SOUTH
	Pass	Pass	1 ♠
Pass	1 NT	Pass	2 ♣
Pass	3 ♣	Pass	3 ♡
Pass	3 ♠	Pass	4 ♠
All Pass			

You may not care for the bidding, but this was at matchpoints –
playing in the major suit was desirable.

West led a diamond to the ace. Declarer began with three
rounds of spades. West won the jack and forced declarer to ruff
a diamond. Unable to play another trump, declarer began to
run the clubs. However, East gave count, and West carefully
waited until the fourth round of clubs to ruff in, stranding
dummy's fifth club. He exited with a diamond, and declarer had
to lose two heart tricks in the end for down one.

Dlr: South   ♠ K Q 4
Vul: Both   ♡ K 7
                    ◇ A 8 6
                    ♣ A 8 5 4 2

♠ 10 8 7   ♠ J 6
♡ J 9 6 4 2   □   ♡ A Q 10 5
◇ 9 7 3 2   ◇ Q J 10
♣ Q   ♣ J 10 7 6

                    ♠ A 9 5 3 2
                    ♡ 8 3
                    ◇ K 5 4
                    ♣ K 9 3

WEST	NORTH	EAST	SOUTH
			Pass
Pass	1 NT	Pass	3 ♠
Pass	4 ♠	All Pass	

On many occasions, an ill-considered ruff costs a trick immediately, and perhaps a tempo as well. On the deal above, West led a heart against 4♠, and East took the ace and queen. Declarer won the ♢Q switch in hand, cashed the ♣K, and played another club. West unwisely ruffed, in effect trumping his partner's winner. A diamond return knocked out the ace, but declarer drew all the trumps with the ace and king, cashed the ♣A, ruffed a club, and returned to dummy with a trump to throw his diamond loser on the good club.

Ruffing in when declarer can follow with a loser usually is the wrong move. If West had patiently discarded on the second club, declarer would have had no chance to make his game.

A frequent reason for refusing to spend a trump involves *control*, another theme that was discussed in Quiz 11.

Dlr: South   ♠ J 6
Vul: None   ♡ K 10 3
                    ♢ A Q 6 5 4 3
                    ♣ 7 2

♠ 10 8 5		♠ K Q 9 7 4
♡ 9 8 6 5	□	♡ J 7
♢ K J		♢ 10 9 8
♣ K 10 8 6		♣ Q 9 4

                    ♠ A 3 2
                    ♡ A Q 4 2
                    ♢ 7 2
                    ♣ A J 5 3

WEST	NORTH	EAST	SOUTH
			1 ♣
Pass	1 ♢	Pass	1 ♡
Pass	2 ♡	Pass	3 ♡
Pass	4 ♡	All Pass	

Despite having only three trumps, North thought he might as well accept partner's game invitation. If diamonds came in and trumps split well 4♡ might make. If not, even 3♡ probably would fail.

Declarer won the opening spade lead, took a successful diamond finesse, and continued with the ◇A and a diamond, ruffed low. West seized the chance to overruff, and that was the end of the defence. Had West now returned a club or heart, declarer could win, draw trumps ending in dummy, and make use of the good diamonds. West actually led to the ♠K and East continued with the ♠9, hoping to force dummy. However, declarer discarded a club, allowing East to win. When East played a fourth spade, his only chance, declarer ruffed low in his hand. Whether West overruffed or discarded, declarer again could draw trumps ending in dummy and run the diamonds.

If West had discarded a club on the third round of diamonds, preserving his trump length, he would have maintained control of the hand. Against continued good defence, declarer would have been unlikely to get home.

Problems

1. Dlr: South
Vul: N-S

♠ K 6 5 2
♡ Q 6 4
◇ K Q 10 2
♣ J 9

□

♠ Q 10 8
♡ K 8 7 5
◇ 9 8 3
♣ K 8 4

WEST	NORTH	EAST	SOUTH
			1 ♣
Pass	1 ◇	Pass	1 ♠
Pass	3 ♠	Pass	4 ♠
All Pass			

West, your partner, leads the ♡J. You cover dummy's queen, and declarer's ace wins. Declarer cashes the ♠A and ♠K; West follows with the jack on the second round. Next come the ◇A, the ◇J, and a diamond to the king, West following all three times. Dummy now leads the ◇Q. How do you defend?

2. Dlr: South   ♠ 10
     Vul: N-S   ♡ 9 4
              ◇ A K J 5 3
              ♣ 10 6 5 4 2

                              ♠ J 8 4 2
               □   ♡ A 6
                              ◇ Q 9 8 4
                              ♣ J 8 7

WEST	NORTH	EAST	SOUTH
			1 ♠
Pass	1 NT	Pass	4 ♠
All Pass			

West, your partner, leads the ♡7. You win and return a heart to the jack and king. When partner leads a low heart at trick three, declarer ruffs with dummy's ♠10. How do you defend?

Solutions

1. If declarer's heart ace were singleton, he would have manoeuvered to ruff both of dummy's hearts before playing trumps. Chances are that his pattern was 4-2-3-4, and he is about to throw the losing heart on the ◇Q. You cannot prevent this, so ruffing with your high trump can't be right. If you hang on to the ♠Q, you should get in to cash it (if declarer had the ♣A, his opening bid would have been 1 NT), and you'd like to draw *two* of declarer's trumps for one.

               ♠ K 6 5 2
               ♡ Q 6 4
               ◇ K Q 10 2
               ♣ J 9

 ♠ J 9   ♠ Q 10 8
 ♡ J 10 9 3   ♡ K 8 7 5
 ◇ 7 6 5   □   ◇ 9 8 3
 ♣ A 6 5 2   ♣ K 8 4

               ♠ A 7 4 3
               ♡ A 2
               ◇ A J 4
               ♣ Q 10 7 3

If you discard, declarer can do no better than lead a club to partner's ace. Partner then forces declarer to ruff a heart. When you win the next club, you draw declarer's last trump and cash a heart for down one.

2. Discard a diamond. You will make the ♠J in any case, and if partner has something good in spades, you may gain a trick by refusing to overruff. The full deal might be:

```
                    ♠ 10
                    ♡ 9 4
                    ◇ A K J 5 3
                    ♣ 10 6 5 4 2
   ♠ Q 7                          ♠ J 8 4 2
   ♡ K 10 8 7 5 2                 ♡ A 6
   ◇ 10 7 2          □            ◇ Q 9 8 4
   ♣ 9 3                          ♣ J 8 7
                    ♠ A K 9 6 5 3
                    ♡ Q J 3
                    ◇ 6
                    ♣ A K Q
```

Problems

3. Dlr: East   ♠ A J 6 4 3 2
    Vul: None   ♡ 9 6 4
                  ◇ A 5
                  ♣ 6 5

                              ♠ K 9 7
                              ♡ Q 8 5
                 □   ◇ 4
                              ♣ A K 10 7 4 2

WEST	NORTH	EAST	SOUTH
		1 ♣	1 ♡
Pass	1 ♠	Pass	2 ◇
Pass	2 ♡	Pass	3 ◇
Pass	4 ♡	All Pass	

West, your partner, leads a low club. Your ace and king score, declarer dropping the queen on the second round while West unblocks the jack. You shift to a trump, and declarer wins the jack. He then embarks on a rather odd line of play: he leads a spade to the ace, ruffs a spade, goes to the ◇A, and ruffs another spade. Now he leads the ◇K. Do you ruff? Why or why not?

4. Dlr: South   ♠ 5
        Vul: N-S   ♡ K 9 8 5
                         ◇ A Q 9 8
                         ♣ A 7 6 2

♠ A J 10 8 7 4
♡ J 7   □
◇ K 3
♣ K 9 3

WEST	NORTH	EAST	SOUTH
			Pass
1 ♠	Dbl	Pass	2 ♡
2 ♠	3 ♡	Pass	4 ♡
All Pass			

You, West, elect to lead the ♠A, and this drops partner's king. How do you continue?

Solutions

3.   ♠ A J 6 4 3 2
                         ♡ 9 6 4
                         ◇ A 5
                         ♣ 6 5

♠ Q 10 5   ♠ K 9 7
♡ 10 3   ♡ Q 8 5
◇ J 10 8 6 3   □   ◇ 4
♣ J 8 3   ♣ A K 10 7 4 2

                         ♠ 8
                         ♡ A K J 7 2
                         ◇ K Q 9 7 2
                         ♣ Q 9

You must discard a club on the ◇K (and discard again if declarer lays down the ◇Q next). If you ruff the ◇K, declarer will take the rest with the aid of dummy's spades no matter what you return.

Assuming partner has the J-9 or J-10 of diamonds, which is a safe bet on declarer's line of play, you can overruff when declarer finally has to lead a losing diamond and ruff it in dummy. Then your trump return will leave declarer with a diamond loser in the end.

4.

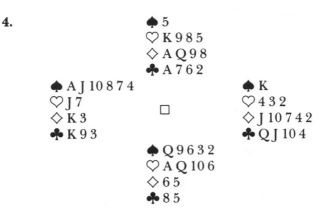

This was board 48 of the 1976 Bermuda Bowl final, United States vs. Italy. The contract and play were the same at both tables. After leading the ♠A, West continued with a low spade. Declarer *discarded* from dummy, allowing East to ruff. He won the club return, drew trumps in two rounds, and wound up with six trump tricks, a spade, a club, and two diamonds.

West's opening lead was not too inspired, but the fatal error was the spade continuation at trick two, which forced East to ruff a loser with his vital third trump. A trump switch by West would have left declarer with no way home.

Quiz 13

Paths in No-trump Defence

As you no doubt know, the play at no-trump often resembles a hundred metre dash between declarer and defence, each of whom is sprinting to establish needed tricks. Generally, the defenders' aim is to set up a long suit, since the declaring side usually has more of the high cards.

The defenders' paucity of high cards also creates another problem – even if someone has winners established, he must get in the lead to cash them. So the defenders always have to keep *preserving communication* in mind – we'll see some examples of this. (See also Quiz 14.)

Ducking a winner to preserve an entry is a common defensive technique.

```
Dlr: South          ♠ Q 9
Vul: N-S            ♡ 7 6 4
                    ◇ A J 7 6 3
                    ♣ K 5 4
    ♠ A 10 7 5 2                    ♠ K 6 3
    ♡ J 8 2                         ♡ Q 10 9 5
    ◇ 8 4            □              ◇ K 9 2
    ♣ 10 8 6                        ♣ J 9 7
                    ♠ J 8 4
                    ♡ A K 3
                    ◇ Q 10 5
                    ♣ A Q 3 2
```

West leads the ♠5 against South's 3 NT. East wins the king and returns the six. When declarer plays the eight, West knows that declarer still has the jack left, for a sure stopper. He therefore allows dummy's queen to win trick two. When East gets in with the ◇K, he will be able to return his last spade, and West can run his suit.

Once in a while, when it is clear that neither side owns a ready source of tricks, the defence may prefer a passive approach. Just as in a passive defence vs. a suit contract, the aim is not to give crucial tricks away by breaking new suits and leading away from honours. (This idea can be especially important at matchpoint duplicate, where the defenders must not concede an overtrick by taking desperate chances trying to defeat an impregnable contract.)

```
Dlr: South        ♠ K 7 5 3
Vul: None         ♡ K 5 4
                  ◇ K 10 3
                  ♣ J 6 3
      ♠ Q 2                      ♠ A 9 8 4
      ♡ Q 8 2          □         ♡ 10 7 3
      ◇ J 7 2                    ◇ Q 8 6 4
      ♣ K 9 8 5 4                ♣ 10 2
                  ♠ J 10 6
                  ♡ A J 9 6
                  ◇ A 9 5
                  ♣ A Q 7
```

South opens 1 NT and is raised to 3 NT. West leads the ♣5 – jack, ten, seven. Declarer tries a heart to the jack, losing to West's queen. West can see that dummy is no powerhouse, and declarer is known to have a balanced hand also. So there is little reason for a desperate move like a switch to the ♠Q – it is best to exit safely with a heart. Let declarer attack the remaining suits.

One other possible defensive approach is neutralizing declarer's source of tricks. The subject is covered fully in Quiz 10, so only one example will be given here.

```
Dlr: North        ♠ K Q 4 3
Vul: Both         ♡ 8 6 3
                  ◇ K Q 10 7 6
                  ♣ Q
      ♠ 7 6 5                    ♠ A J 10 8
      ♡ Q 9 7          □         ♡ 10 5 2
      ◇ 8                        ◇ A 5 4 2
      ♣ 9 8 7 6 5 2              ♣ A 10
                  ♠ 9 2
                  ♡ A K J 4
                  ◇ J 9 3
                  ♣ K J 4 3
```

WEST	NORTH	EAST	SOUTH
	1 ◇	Pass	1 ♡
Pass	1 ♠	Pass	3 NT
All Pass			

West leads the ♣9 to the queen and ace. If East merely returns a club, declarer wins, knocks out the ◇A, and reaches dummy with a spade to cash the diamonds. He can take four diamonds, two clubs, two hearts, and a spade.

Instead, East should turn his attention to isolating the diamond suit. This can be done easily by returning the ♠J. Declarer's entry to dummy is dislodged before he is ready to use it, and the best he can do is make eight tricks.

Problems

1. Dlr: South
　　Vul: Both

　　　　　　　♠ J 3
　　　　　　　♡ A J 4
　　　　　　　◇ A 10 8 5 3
　　　　　　　♣ K 7 6

♠ K 9 7 4 2
♡ 10 5 3
◇ 7 6 　　　　□
♣ 9 4 2

WEST	NORTH	EAST	SOUTH
			1 ♣
Pass	1 ◇	Pass	1 NT
Pass	3 NT		

You, West, lead the ♠4. Dummy plays the jack, and partner, to your relief, covers with the queen. Declarer plays the ♠6 at trick one and follows with the eight when East continues with the ♠10. Plan your defence.

2. Dlr: South
　　Vul: N-S

　　　　　　　♠ 8 7
　　　　　　　♡ A K J 8 6
　　　　　　　◇ J 10 9
　　　　　　　♣ Q 3 2

♠ Q J 10
♡ 5 4 3
◇ A Q 7 3 　　□
♣ K 10 6

WEST	NORTH	EAST	SOUTH
			1 ◇
Pass	1 ♡	Pass	1 NT
Pass	3 NT	All Pass	

You, West, try the ♠Q – seven, nine, five. You continue with the ♠J – eight, four, six. What next?

Solutions

1. Overtake with the ♠K and shift to the ♡10. You have no entry, so establishing the spades is fruitless. However, with that five-card diamond suit in dummy you can't afford to go passive. Perhaps partner has something good in hearts, plus an entry in diamonds.

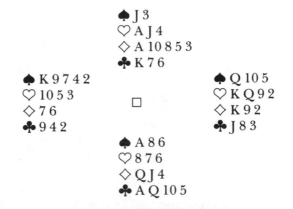

```
              ♠ J 3
              ♡ A J 4
              ◇ A 10 8 5 3
              ♣ K 7 6
♠ K 9 7 4 2                ♠ Q 10 5
♡ 10 5 3                   ♡ K Q 9 2
◇ 7 6          □           ◇ K 9 2
♣ 9 4 2                    ♣ J 8 3
              ♠ A 8 6
              ♡ 8 7 6
              ◇ Q J 4
              ♣ A Q 10 5
```

2. Declarer is certain to have at least four diamonds to the king plus the ♡Q, so he has the material for nine tricks. But your partner cannot have an entry to his spades – you must look elsewhere for defensive tricks. Clubs are the only chance. You have to play East for the ♣J and switch to a club at trick three.

♠ 8 7
♡ A K J 8 6
◇ J 10 9
♣ Q 3 2

♠ Q J 10   ♠ K 9 4 3 2
♡ 5 4 3   □   ♡ 7 2
◇ A Q 7 3   ◇ 6 2
♣ K 10 6   ♣ J 9 8 7

♠ A 6 5
♡ Q 10 9
◇ K 8 5 4
♣ A 5 4

There is one other point – if you do not lead the ♣K at trick three, you must unblock it if declarer cashes the ♣A later; otherwise you could find yourself subjected to an end-play.

Problems

3. Dlr: South   ♠ Q 10 6 3
    Vul: N-S   ♡ J 6
                       ◇ K Q 4
                       ♣ 10 8 6 3
                              ♠ 9 7 2
                       □   ♡ 10 7 3
                              ◇ J 10 7 3
                              ♣ A 4 2

WEST	NORTH	EAST	SOUTH
			1 ♣
Pass	1 ♠	Pass	2 NT
Pass	3 NT	All Pass	

West, your partner, leads the ♡5. Dummy's jack wins, declarer playing the four. At trick two, a low club is led from dummy. How do you defend?

4.   Dlr: South ♠ A 8 4 2
  Vul: E-W ♡ 8 5 3
      ♢ K 5
      ♣ Q 10 9 5

♠ 9 6
♡ J 9 6
♢ Q 10 8 7 3 □
♣ A 8 3

WEST	NORTH	EAST	SOUTH
			1 ♣
Pass	1 ♠	Pass	2 NT
Pass	3 NT	All Pass	

You, West, lead the ♢7. Declarer wins the king in dummy, partner playing the nine. Declarer continues with a club from dummy – four, king. Quickly now: Do you take this trick? If you take it, what do you lead next?

Solutions

3.   Go right in with the ♣A and return a heart. The idea is to spend your entry early so you can establish partner's suit while his (hoped-for) entry is preserved. The full deal:

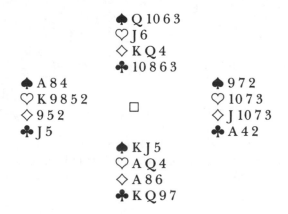

     ♠ Q 10 6 3
     ♡ J 6
     ♢ K Q 4
     ♣ 10 8 6 3

♠ A 8 4   ♠ 9 7 2
♡ K 9 8 5 2   ♡ 10 7 3
♢ 9 5 2   □ ♢ J 10 7 3
♣ J 5   ♣ A 4 2

     ♠ K J 5
     ♡ A Q 4
     ♢ A 8 6
     ♣ K Q 9 7

On this layout, if declarer sneaks by with one club trick, he will switch promptly to spades for nine tricks. Rising with the ♣A also would be necessary if declarer's hand were

♠ A K x
♡ K x x
◇ A x x
♣ K Q x x

4. Let the ♣K hold. Of course, you won't gain a club trick if declarer also has the jack. However, you might induce him to switch suits if he thinks your partner has the ♣A and you have an entry somewhere else.

Another possible benefit is illustrated by the actual deal:

```
                    ♠ A 8 4 2
                    ♡ 8 5 3
                    ◇ K 5
                    ♣ Q 10 9 5
  ♠ 9 6                            ♠ J 10 7 3
  ♡ J 9 6                          ♡ Q 10 2
  ◇ Q 10 8 7 3        □           ◇ J 9 4
  ♣ A 8 3                          ♣ J 7 4
                    ♠ K Q 5
                    ♡ A K 7 4
                    ◇ A 6 2
                    ♣ K 6 2
```

After the ♣K wins, declarer surely will continue with a club to the nine and jack. East returns a diamond, and your suit is set up while you still have your entry! If you win the ♣A, you can establish diamonds, all right. But declarer will lose a club finesse to your partner's jack, win the return, and cash out his nine tricks.

Your *tempo* is a definite factor in a situation like this. *If you huddle over your play to trick two, you might as well go ahead and win the ace.* You need to make up your mind in advance that you will cling to your entry until the time is ripe.

Quiz 14

Communication: Keeping Yours, Cutting Theirs

Entries are the means by which one defender or the other gains the lead. Since the defenders usually have fewer entries than declarer, they often must take special measures to keep their communications intact. This is especially true in no-trump defence, where establishing and cashing long cards is frequently the goal. (See Quiz 13.)

Look at this deal:

```
Dlr: North        ♠ K 6
Vul: None         ♡ 8 3
                  ◇ A K 5
                  ♣ K 10 8 6 4 2

♠ Q 7 5 4 2                      ♠ 10 9 8
♡ 9 2                            ♡ A K Q 7 4
◇ 8 7 3           □              ◇ Q 10 6
♣ Q J 9                          ♣ 5 3

                  ♠ A J 3
                  ♡ J 10 6 5
                  ◇ J 9 4 2
                  ♣ A 7
```

North opens 1♣, East overcalls 1♡, South jumps to 2NT (invitational), and North goes on to 3 NT. West leads the ♡9.

East knows that the contract is cold unless West has a trick in clubs. Even so, declarer will prevail unless the defence can cash four heart tricks when West gets in. Clearing the heart suit will not help, since East has no fast entry on the side. Since, on the bidding, declarer is known to have one heart stopper anyway, East *ducks* the first heart, signalling with the seven.

A slightly more advanced case of keeping communication:

Dlr: North
Vul: Both

```
                    ♠ 5 4 3
                    ♡ A Q 2
                    ◇ Q J 10 8 3
                    ♣ A 3
    ♠ 10 2                          ♠ K Q 9 8 7
    ♡ 10 9 5 4          □          ♡ J 6 3
    ◇ K 2                           ◇ A 6
    ♣ 10 8 7 6 5                    ♣ 9 4 2
                    ♠ A J 6
                    ♡ K 8 7
                    ◇ 9 7 5 4
                    ♣ K Q J
```

WEST	NORTH	EAST	SOUTH
	1 ◇	1 ♠	3 NT
All Pass			

When West leads the ♣10, East must play the *nine*. If he puts up
an honour, declarer *ducks* and wins the second round. The
defenders are now out of touch, and declarer has time to knock
out both diamond honours, making an overtrick.

However, if declarer is forced to take one of his sure spade
winners at trick one, West can jump in with the ◇K when
declarer leads that suit. When West returns his second spade,
East's spades will be set up while he still has the ◇A.

Of course, ruining *declarer's* communication is a technique that
the defenders also must employ. Here is a simple example.

Dlr: South
Vul: Both

```
                    ♠ 6 4
                    ♡ 6 5 3
                    ◇ A Q
                    ♣ K J 10 7 6 3
    ♠ J 9 8 5                        ♠ Q 10 3
    ♡ J 9 7 4 2        □            ♡ A 8
    ◇ 8 7 6                          ◇ 9 5 4 3 2
    ♣ 2                             ♣ A Q 4
                    ♠ A K 7 2
                    ♡ K Q 10
                    ◇ K J 10
                    ♣ 9 8 5
```

South opened 1 NT and was raised to 3 NT. West led a heart to

East's ace, but East knew that partner couldn't have an established suit plus an entry. Instead of returning a heart, East switched to diamonds, attacking declarer's entries. Declarer won in hand and finessed in clubs, but when East won the queen, another diamond play severed declarer's last link with dummy. East held up his ♣A until the third round and exited with a spade – declarer had to lose two more tricks for down one.

In the 1979 Bermuda Bowl, Benito Garozzo of Italy produced a classic defence.

Dlr: South   ♠ Q J 7 3 2
Vul: Both   ♡ J 10 2
                    ◇ A Q 8
                    ♣ K J

♠ 8 4   ♠ K 10 9 6 5
♡ Q 8 7 3   ♡ A 5
◇ 10 4   □   ◇ 9 6 5
♣ A 7 6 4 2   ♣ 8 5 3

                    ♠ A
                    ♡ K 9 6 4
                    ◇ K J 7 3 2
                    ♣ Q 10 9

At one table, Italy's South went down in 3NT, adopting an inferior line of play. In the replay:

WEST	NORTH	EAST	SOUTH
Lauria	*Brachman*	*Garozzo*	*Passell*
			1 ◇
Pass	1 ♠	Pass	1 NT
Pass	2 ♣[1]	Pass	2 ♡
Pass	3 NT	All Pass	

[1] artificial force (Crowhurst Convention)

West started the ♣2 (playing 'attitude' leads). Declarer won and correctly cashed the ♠A, then went to the ◇Q and led the ♠Q to East's king. What should East play now?

Even looking at all four hands, the winning defence is hardly obvious. Most Easts would return a club without much thought. A few might try the ♠10 or a sneaky low heart. Garozzo's choice was a diamond – a play so full of subtlety that one is apt to ponder what manner of thought processes inspired it.

Declarer's transportation was damaged just the slightest bit. Naturally enough, he won the ♢A and cashed the ♠J, not knowing about the 5-2 spade break. Garozzo now won three spade tricks and the ♡A, and West's ♣A was the setting trick. No swing!

For more on getting declarer all tangled up, see Quiz 10.

Problems

1. Dlr: North ♠ A J 6
    Vul: None ♡ A 8
            ♢ K J 9 6 5 2
            ♣ J 5

                        ♠ 10 9 8 3
            □   ♡ K J 6
                        ♢ A Q 4
                        ♣ K 9 6

WEST	NORTH	EAST	SOUTH
	1 ♢	Pass	1 ♠
Pass	2 ♢	Pass	2 NT
Pass	3 ♣	Pass	3 NT
All Pass			

West, your partner, leads the ♡5. Plan your defence.

2. Dlr: South ♠ K Q
    Vul: N-S ♡ J 6 3
           ♢ Q J 10 7 6
           ♣ K 4 3

                      ♠ A 7 3
           □   ♡ 10 9 7 5 4
                      ♢ 8 5 4
                      ♣ 9 8

WEST	NORTH	EAST	SOUTH
			1 NT
Pass	3 NT	All Pass	

West, your partner, leads the ♣2. Plan your defence.

Solutions

1.

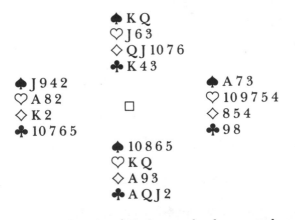

♠ A J 6
♥ A 8
♦ K J 9 6 5 2
♣ J 5

♠ Q 5
♥ 10 9 5 4 2
♦ 8 7
♣ 10 8 7 3

♠ 10 9 8 3
♥ K J 6
♦ A Q 4
♣ K 9 6

♠ K 7 4 2
♥ Q 7 3
♦ 10 3
♣ A Q 4 2

Declarer surely will play a low heart from dummy, and you need to insert the *jack*. On the bidding, West can have no more than a queen. If he has the ♥Q, it doesn't matter which honour you play. But if partner's hearts are headed by the ten, the only way to preserve your communication is to let declarer win the queen at trick one.

When you take the ♦Q, you will return the ♥K. Then maybe partner's hearts will run when you get in with the ♦A.

2.   Duck the first trick, signalling with the seven. This is one time when it would not be a good idea to expend your entry at an early stage.

♠ K Q
♥ J 6 3
♦ Q J 10 7 6
♣ K 4 3

♠ J 9 4 2
♥ A 8 2
♦ K 2
♣ 10 7 6 5

♠ A 7 3
♥ 10 9 7 5 4
♦ 8 5 4
♣ 9 8

♠ 10 8 6 5
♥ K Q
♦ A 9 3
♣ A Q J 2

When partner wins the ♦K, he can lead a second spade. Now you take the ace and return a spade through declarer, for five tricks in all.

Problems

3. Dlr: North   ♠ A Q 2
     Vul: N-S   ♡ K 4
              ◇ Q J 10 8 6
              ♣ A K 5

                           ♠ K 9 5
                   □   ♡ A Q J 7 5
                           ◇ 5 3
                           ♣ 10 7 6

WEST	NORTH	EAST	SOUTH
	1 ◇	1 ♡	Pass
Pass	Dbl	Pass	1 NT
Pass	2 NT	Pass	3 NT
All Pass			

West, your partner, leads the ♡9. Plan your defence.

4. Dlr: South   ♠ A 8 6
     Vul: Both   ♡ J 9 5 3
              ◇ J 8 2
              ♣ K Q 5

   ♠ K 9 5
   ♡ Q 10 6 2
   ◇ A Q 4 3   □
   ♣ 10 7

WEST	NORTH	EAST	SOUTH
			1 ◇
Pass	1 ♡	Pass	1 NT
Pass	2 NT	All Pass	

You, West, lead the ♠5. Dummy plays low, and East's queen wins. Declarer plays the jack on the ♠2 return and ducks your king. Partner and declarer both follow to the third round of spades, dummy's ace winning. At trick four, declarer passes dummy's ◇8 to your queen, East playing the seven. What do you lead now?

Solutions

3.   This deal is a relative of the second one in the introduction to this Quiz. You know declarer has one heart stopper, so you must duck the first trick completely to keep alive your chances of running the whole heart suit. The full deal is:

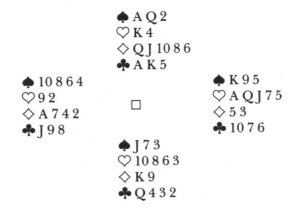

```
              ♠ A Q 2
              ♡ K 4
              ◇ Q J 10 8 6
              ♣ A K 5
♠ 10 8 6 4                    ♠ K 9 5
♡ 9 2                         ♡ A Q J 7 5
◇ A 7 4 2        □            ◇ 5 3
♣ J 9 8                       ♣ 10 7 6
              ♠ J 7 3
              ♡ 10 8 6 3
              ◇ K 9
              ♣ Q 4 3 2
```

4.   If you can find a way to get East in the lead, you should collect three spade tricks, his entry and two diamonds. But there is no time to waste – declarer is likely to have a five-card diamond suit, and he'll set up eight tricks if you defend passively.

    There is no problem if partner has an ace, but he could have the ♡K. In that case, you can't succeed by leading a low heart. With the nine a threat in dummy, you must lead the *queen*. The full deal:

```
              ♠ A 8 6
              ♡ J 9 5 3
              ◇ J 8 2
              ♣ K Q 5
♠ K 9 5                      ♠ Q 10 7 2
♡ Q 10 6 2                   ♡ K 8 7
◇ A Q 4 3        □           ◇ 7
♣ 10 7                       ♣ J 9 8 4 3
              ♠ J 4 3
              ♡ A 4
              ◇ K 10 9 6 5
              ♣ A 6 2
```

This is the Deschapelles Coup, the sacrifice of a high card to create an entry in partner's hand. Note what will happen if you lead a low heart.

Quiz 15

Talk to Partner: Defensive Signals

Most readers will be familiar with the three types of standard defensive signals. I list them here according to the priority of their use.

1.   *Attitude* signals encourage or discourage the lead of a suit. A high card encourages, a low one shows apathy, discourages or, in some situations, may demand a shift. Attitude is shown when discarding or when partner is leading a suit.

2.   *Count* signals tell partner how many cards you have in a suit. A high-low sequence of plays shows an even number of cards, low-high shows an odd number. With rare exceptions, this signal is used as *declarer* leads a suit.

3.   **Suit-preference** signals, which arise only in special situations, are unusual in that they convey a message about a suit other than the one being played. Under the right circumstances, the play of an *unusually* high card draws attention to a high-ranking suit; an *unusually* low card shows interest in a low-ranking suit.

Suit-preference signals, though extremely useful, often are over-used or abused. In fact, good judgment is needed to use *any* signal efficiently.

```
Dlr: East          ♠ A J 7
Vul: None          ♡ K 6 4 3
                   ◇ K Q 10 7
                   ♣ Q 5
     ♠ 9 8 4 2                    ♠ K Q 10
     ♡ 5                          ♡ 8 7
     ◇ 9 6 4 3        □           ◇ A 8
     ♣ A 9 6 3                    ♣ K J 10 7 4 2
                   ♠ 6 5 3
                   ♡ A Q J 10 9 2
                   ◇ J 5 2
                   ♣ 8
```

WEST	NORTH	EAST	SOUTH
		1 ♣	2 ♡
Pass	4 ♡	All Pass	

If West leads the ♣A, East should play the discouraging *two*. Since East obviously has a wide choice of cards to signal with, this play practically orders West to lead something else. A spade is the obvious switch.

Principle: The purpose of a signal is to *direct the defence*, not to confirm or deny certain high cards. We will see this principle over and over again.

Dlr: South   ♠ J 9 2
Vul: N-S   ♡ J 10 3
                ◇ K Q 4
                ♣ Q 7 6 3

♠ A Q 7 6 3   ♠ 8 4
♡ K 2   □   ♡ 9 8 7 6 4
◇ 8 7   ◇ 10 9 3
♣ J 8 4 2   ♣ A 10 9

                ♠ K 10 5
                ♡ A Q 5
                ◇ A J 6 5 2
                ♣ K 5

On this deal, E-W can employ the count signal. West leads the ♠6 against 3 NT. Declarer wins the jack on dummy, dropping a sneaky ten from his hand. He then passes the ♡J to West's king.

Q: How does West know not to lay down the ♠A?

A: East should have played the ♠8 at trick one, denying three cards.

(Yes, attitude signals take precedence over count. But East's attitude about spades is known when he can't beat dummy's jack, so this becomes a count situation.) Knowing declarer still has the guarded ♠K, West can switch and avoid giving up the ninth trick.

A different procedure is used when giving count in the trump suit – using a high trump to signal a doubleton might be wasteful. Play high-low in trumps to show three (or five).

Here is a deal that illustrates the use of this *trump echo* as well as a common suit-preference situation.

Dlr: West   ♠ J 4
Vul: Both   ♡ K 9 4 3
                  ◇ A K Q 4
                  ♣ 6 5 3

♠ A 7 2   ♠ 8 6 3
♡ A Q 8 6 2   ♡ 5
◇ 7   □   ◇ J 10 8 6 2
♣ A 9 4 2   ♣ J 10 8 7

                ♠ K Q 10 9 5
                ♡ J 10 7
                ◇ 9 5 3
                ♣ K Q

WEST	NORTH	EAST	SOUTH
1 ♡	Pass	Pass	1 ♠
All Pass			

N-S bid very conservatively – as it turned out, they'd have been as well off in 3 NT, even with a club lead.

West led his singleton diamond, and East dropped the jack when dummy won. East played the six on the first trump lead, and West won. He played ♡A and ♡Q, East ruffing with the three. The play continued with the ◇10, ruffed; the ♡8 ruffed by East; another diamond ruff. The ♣A was the setting trick.

Let's re-examine the defender's plays:

Trick one: East's ◇J was suit preference, suggesting the lead of the higher-ranking of the other suits (except trumps, which normally are excluded).

Trick two: East followed with his middle spot card in trumps, starting an echo to show the count.

Trick three: West obediently switched to hearts.

Trick four: West's ♡Q was suit preference, asking for a diamond return. East ruffed with the three, confirming three trumps.

Trick five: East returned the ◇10, suit preference for another heart play.

Trick six: West returned the ♡8 (the highest one he had left), suit preference for diamonds.

Here is suit preference used at no-trump.

Dlr: South
Vul: None

```
                    ♠ 8 6 5 3
                    ♡ K 5
                    ◇ A Q 7 4
                    ♣ 8 7 4
♠ A Q 10                              ♠ 9 4 2
♡ J 9 7 6 2          □               ♡ A Q 8 3
◇ 8 3                                ◇ J 10 6 5
♣ 10 6 3                             ♣ J 2
                    ♠ K J 7
                    ♡ 10 4
                    ◇ K 9 2
                    ♣ A K Q 9 5
```

WEST	NORTH	EAST	SOUTH
			1 NT
Pass	2 NT	Pass	3 NT
All Pass			

West led the ♡6 and dummy's king lost to the ace. When East cashed the ♡Q, West dropped the *jack*. This striking play was an unmistakable suit-preference signal, so East shifted to a spade. West won and put East back in with the ♡8. A spade return completed a four-trick set.

Not all signalling situations admit to such easy interpretation. Suppose a suit is distributed like this:

```
                J 9 3
K Q 6 5          □               A 8 2
                10 7 4
```

West leads the king. In theory, East can afford to play the two to give count, since West will know who has the ace when the king holds the trick. (With the jack in dummy, declarer would not duck if he had the ace.) But what if East wants partner to shift? This is one of many positions that require partnership discussion.

Most signalling headaches result from confusion over suit preference.

Dlr: West   ♠ K 8 5 3
Vul: None   ♡ K 4
                  ◇ 8 6 3
                  ♣ A K J 10

                            ♠ 7 4
                            ♡ J 9 5 2
                  □   ◇ A Q 5
                            ♣ 9 8 6 3

WEST	NORTH	EAST	SOUTH
1 ♡	Dbl	2 ♡	3 ♠
Pass	4 ♠	All Pass	

West leads the ♡A. What should East play? The answer is based on the *priorities* with which the three types of signals are used. Attitude, we said, always takes precedence. If East sticks to that principle, he will play the *two*. When West looks at dummy, the right switch will be apparent.

Some players like suit preference so much that they would lead a *club* when East played his lowest heart. This is contrary to our principles (not to mention illogical, looking at the strong clubs in dummy).

How about this hand?

Dlr: West   ♠ K 9 6 5
Vul: None   ♡ J 10 4
                  ◇ Q 5 4
                  ♣ Q 5 4

♠ A J 10 8 2   ♠ Q 7 3
♡ Q 6   ♡ 8 2
◇ K 9 2   □   ◇ A J 10 3
♣ K 9 7   ♣ 10 8 6 3

                    ♠ 4
                    ♡ A K 9 7 5 3
                    ◇ 8 7 6
                    ♣ A J 2

WEST	NORTH	EAST	SOUTH
1 ♠	Pass	2 ♠	3 ♡
All Pass			

If West leads the ♠A, East should play the queen. A

suit-preference signal is needed here. Declarer is about to obtain a discard on the ♠K; but a look at dummy suggests no *obvious* switch, so attitude alone won't get the job done.

In many instances, the bidding may wind up affecting the interpretation of your signals.

```
Dlr: South          ♠ J 10 6 2
Vul: ?              ♡ A 4 3
                    ◇ Q 7 5
                    ♣ 8 7 2
    ♠ 9 3                            ♠ 8 4
    ♡ 8 7                            ♡ K Q 10 2
    ◇ A K 10 6 2       □            ◇ J 9 4 3
    ♣ K J 5 3                        ♣ 10 9 6
                    ♠ A K Q 7 5
                    ♡ J 9 6 5
                    ◇ 8
                    ♣ A Q 4
```

WEST	NORTH	EAST	SOUTH
			1 ♠
2 ◇	2 ♣	Pass	3 ♠
All Pass			

When West leads the ◇A, East must play the three. Any other card might look like the beginning of a high-low with a doubleton and induce a fatal diamond continuation. There is no way East can show count here – West can only interpret his partner's play as attitude.

Should West interpret East's low-diamond play as asking for a shift to dummy's weak suit, clubs? No, dummy is flat and weak, so *no* shift is urgently needed. (Compare with the previous hand, where dummy had very strong clubs.) West should shift to a trump.

Now suppose neither side is vulnerable, and the bidding is:

WEST	NORTH	EAST	SOUTH
			1 ♠
2 ◇	2 ♣	3 ◇	3 ♠
All Pass			

This time East can play the jack or nine (count), since West knows it cannot be from a doubleton.

West may or may not find the heart switch – he is likely to exit passively with a trump again. However, say only N-S are vulnerable and the bidding is:

WEST	NORTH	EAST	SOUTH
			1 ♠
2 ◇	2 ♠	4 ◇[1]	4 ♠
All Pass			

[1] Pre-emptive, suggesting a sacrifice

Now East is known to have four diamonds, so his play of a high diamond can have suit-preference significance.

The problems in this Quiz include several extensions of the various signals.

Problems

1. Dlr: South   ♠ K 6 4
    Vul: N-S   ♡ 6 5 3
              ◇ K Q J 10 4
              ♣ 6 4

♠ 10 9 8 5 2
♡ K 10 2
◇ A   □
♣ K 10 7 2

WEST	NORTH	EAST	SOUTH
			1 NT
Pass	3 NT	All Pass	

You, West, lead the ♠10 to the four, three, and jack. At trick two, declarer plays the ◇3. You take your ace, partner playing the nine. How do you continue?

2. Dlr: South   ♠ 7 6
    Vul: N-S   ♡ Q 7 3
                ◇ J 6 3
                ♣ Q 10 8 4 2

                           ♠ 10
             □   ♡ A J 9 5
                           ◇ Q 9 8 5
                           ♣ K J 6 5

WEST	NORTH	EAST	SOUTH
			2 ♣
Pass	2 ◇	Pass	2 ♠
Pass	2 NT	Pass	4 ♠
All Pass			

West, your partner, leads the ♣7 – dummy ducks, and your jack forces declarer's ace. Declarer plays off the four top trumps, partner following with the five, four, three, and two while you shed your three fives. Next the ♣9 is led. Partner follows and you take your king. What do you return?

Solutions

1. When declarer obviously will have no trouble running diamonds, it makes no sense for East to show count. The ◇9 should be suit preference, so switch to hearts.

                 ♠ K 6 4
                 ♡ 6 5 3
                 ◇ K Q J 10 4
                 ♣ 6 4

♠ 10 9 8 5 2   ♠ 3
♡ K 10 2   □   ♡ A J 9 8 4
◇ A   ◇ 9 5 2
♣ K 10 7 2   ♣ 9 8 5 3

                 ♠ A Q J 7
                 ♡ Q 7
                 ◇ 8 7 6 3
                 ♣ A Q J

2.

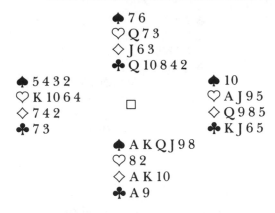

♠ 7 6
♡ Q 7 3
◇ J 6 3
♣ Q 10 8 4 2

♠ 5 4 3 2   ♠ 10
♡ K 10 6 4   ♡ A J 9 5
◇ 7 4 2   ◇ Q 9 8 5
♣ 7 3   ♣ K J 6 5

♠ A K Q J 9 8
♡ 8 2
◇ A K 10
♣ A 9

Lead a low heart. Declarer won't have less than six spades on this bidding, so West wasn't showing count with his high-low play in trumps – he was improvising a suit-preference signal. How else could he suggest which red suit you should lead if you won a club trick?

Problems

3. Dlr: South   ♠ A 4
**   Vul: E-W**   ♡ K Q 7 4
                           ◇ 7 6 3
                           ♣ J 6 5 2

♠ J 9 5 2
♡ A 5 3
◇ J 9 5 2
♣ 8 3

WEST	NORTH	EAST	SOUTH
			1 NT
Pass	2 ♣	Pass	2 ◇
Pass	3 NT	All Pass	

Declarer ducks your ♠2 opening lead to East's king, and the ♠3 is returned to dummy's ace. Declarer has followed with the six and ten. At trick three, a heart is led to the eight and jack, and you duck. Next comes the ♡6. How do you defend?

4. Dlr: East
    Vul: N-S

♠ 6 5
♡ K J 9 5
◇ 10 6 5
♣ K 10 9 5

♠ Q 9 3
♡ 10 6 4 2
◇ K J
♣ J 8 6 2

☐

WEST	NORTH	EAST	SOUTH
		1 ◇	1 ♠
Dbl¹	Pass	2 ◇	2 ♠
3 ◇	3 ♠	All Pass	

¹ negative

You are West. Both your 3◇ bid and North's 3♠ were questionable, but that's all in the past. You lead the ◇K, winning and continue with the ◇J. East takes the ace and continues with the ◇Q. Declarer ruffs with the seven, and you overruff with the nine. How do you continue?

Solutions

3. You must duck the second heart. East's eight can't be the start of a high-low sequence with four cards. He would play the ten from 10-9-8-2.

♠ A 4
♡ K Q 7 4
◇ 7 6 3
♣ J 6 5 2

♠ J 9 5 2
♡ A 5 3
◇ J 9 5 2
♣ 8 3

☐

♠ K 8 7 3
♡ 10 9 8
◇ Q 10
♣ Q 10 9 7

♠ Q 10 6
♡ J 6 2
◇ A K 8 4
♣ A K 4

4.   Lead the ♡10. East did not have suit preference available at trick three – he had to lead a card to beat dummy. However, he had options at trick *two*. When he won the ◇A rather than the queen, he showed a liking for hearts.

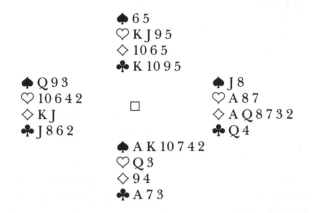

```
                    ♠ 6 5
                    ♡ K J 9 5
                    ◇ 10 6 5
                    ♣ K 10 9 5
♠ Q 9 3                          ♠ J 8
♡ 10 6 4 2          □            ♡ A 8 7
◇ K J                            ◇ A Q 8 7 3 2
♣ J 8 6 2                        ♣ Q 4
                    ♠ A K 10 7 4 2
                    ♡ Q 3
                    ◇ 9 4
                    ♣ A 7 3
```

After East wins the ♡A, a fourth round of diamonds promotes the setting trick in trumps.

Quiz 16
Judicious Discards

Since the defenders have to make some discards on practically every hand, it's surprising that the literature on the subject is relatively lean. (Only Hugh Kelsey, in his excellent *More Killing Defence*, has been willing to tackle the subject in great depth.) Probably, this is because discarding can be such a big headache. Delicate reasoning often is required, and even expert partnerships can fall at a difficult hurdle. Discarding is not an easy subject to write about systematically.

Most discards fall into two broad categories. *Informative* discards give partner useful information – you can indicate a sequential holding, or show attitude, count, or suit preference. *Tactical* discards include those which unblock a suit, create an entry, or deceive declarer.

```
                  ♠ K 4 3
                  ♡ 8 3
                  ◇ K 10 7 6 3
                  ♣ K 4 3
  ♠ J 10 6                      ♠ Q 9 8 2
  ♡ A 10 7 6 5        □         ♡ Q 9 4 2
  ◇ Q 8 4                       ◇ 2
  ♣ J 10                        ♣ Q 9 8 5
                  ♠ A 7 5
                  ♡ K J
                  ◇ A J 9 5
                  ♣ A 7 6 2
```

West leads the ♡6 against 3 NT, and declarer takes East's queen with the king. He plays a diamond to the king and a diamond back. East should discard the ♡2, suggesting an original holding of four hearts. When West wins a diamond trick, he will know it is correct to play the ♡A. This is a simple informative discard.

If East's hearts were Q-9-4, he might discard the ♡9, suggesting three hearts, and West would lead a black suit, hoping partner could get in and lead a heart through. (If East started with only two hearts, he obviously would not throw away his last one.)

Many discarding problems involve simply trying to decide which winners or potential winners to keep.

```
Dlr: South              ♠ 8 5 3
Vul: Both               ♡ A J 7 3
                        ◇ Q J 6 5
                        ♣ 8 7
        ♠ K Q J 9 7                      ♠ 6 2
        ♡ Q 6                            ♡ 10 9 4 2
        ◇ 10 9 7          □              ◇ 8 4 2
        ♣ A 6 5                          ♣ J 10 9 2
                        ♠ A 10 4
                        ♡ K 8 5
                        ◇ A K 3
                        ♣ K Q 4 3
```

WEST	NORTH	EAST	SOUTH
			1 ♣
1 ♠	Dbl	Pass	2 NT
Pass	3 NT	All Pass	

Declarer wins the second spade and plays four rounds of diamonds. What should East's discard be? He should not throw a heart, on the principle that it is right to keep parity with dummy's length. Is it not dangerous to throw a club when declarer has bid the suit? No, declarer has nine tricks anyway if his hand is

$$\begin{align}
&♠ A x x \\
&♡ x x x \\
&◇ A K x \\
&♣ A K Q x,
\end{align}$$

and if he holds

$$\begin{align}
&♠ A x x \\
&♡ x x \\
&◇ A K x \\
&♣ A K x x x
\end{align}$$

he always is down.

There is nothing worse than being subjected to a long string of declarer's winners and knowing that a wrong discard is certain to give the contract away. Luckily, many such problems can be solved by logical reasoning or by drawing inferences from the bidding or play. On the following deal, only overtricks were at stake.

```
                    ♠ K J 6 3
                    ♡ 8 7 3
                    ◇ 9 6 5 2
                    ♣ 6 5
  ♠ 5                                    ♠ 9 8 4
  ♡ Q 10 6 2                             ♡ J 9 5 4
  ◇ Q 10 8 4         □                   ◇ J 7
  ♣ Q J 10 4                             ♣ A 9 3 2
                    ♠ A Q 10 7 2
                    ♡ A K
                    ◇ A K 3
                    ♣ K 8 7
```

South played in 4♠, and West led the ♣Q. East won the ace and returned a club to declarer's king. Declarer ruffed a club high and ran his trumps. On the last trump, West must unguard one of the red suits. What should he keep?

West knows that declarer started with five spades and three clubs. If declarer had four diamonds and one heart, East might have returned his singleton diamond at trick two. If declarer had four hearts and one diamond, he would have played off ace, king, and another heart before drawing trumps, intending to ruff the fourth heart if necessary.

Assuming that declarer has three cards in one red suit and two in the other, West should keep *diamonds*. The reason is very simple: If declarer has a diamond loser, only West can guard the suit. Let East protect hearts.

Dlr: South   ♠ A J 4
Vul: None   ♡ K 10 3
                    ◇ 6 5 2
                    ♣ A J 10 4

♠ 5 3 2   ♠ K 7
♡ 7 6 5   ♡ Q 9 8 4
◇ Q J 9   □   ◇ K 8 7 4
♣ Q 8 3 2   ♣ K 9 5

                    ♠ Q 10 9 8 6
                    ♡ A J 2
                    ◇ A 10 3
                    ♣ 7 6

WEST	NORTH	EAST	SOUTH
			Pass
Pass	1 ♣	Pass	1 ♠
Pass	2 ♠	Pass	2 NT
Pass	3 NT	All Pass	

West led the ◇Q. Declarer held up twice, won the third diamond and passed the ♠10 to East's king. The good diamond was cashed, everybody discarding clubs. East then exited safely with his remaining spade.

The defenders should have had few problems discarding on the run of the spades. Declarer soon was known to have four spade tricks, plus two heart tricks (if East had the ♡A, he would have cashed it for the setting trick) and one each in diamonds and clubs. South couldn't have the ♣K, which would give him 14 HCP and an opening bid, not to mention an obvious claim for the rest. West, however, thought he needed to keep the ♣Q guarded. After he discarded two hearts, declarer successfully played East for the ♡Q.

The defenders might have done better if West had thrown two more clubs, saving his three small hearts, while East discarded two hearts (!) and a club.

Expert defenders are aware that declarer may draw inferences from their discards, and they sometimes try to deceive him. This fine deal arose in the 1967 Bermuda Bowl.

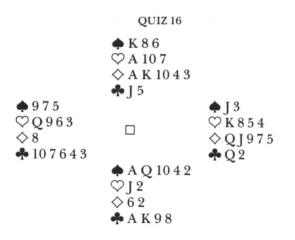

♠ K 8 6
♡ A 10 7
◇ A K 10 4 3
♣ J 5

♠ 9 7 5
♡ Q 9 6 3
◇ 8
♣ 10 7 6 4 3

♠ J 3
♡ K 8 5 4
◇ Q J 9 7 5
♣ Q 2

♠ A Q 10 4 2
♡ J 2
◇ 6 2
♣ A K 9 8

Pietro Forquet and Benito Garozzo of Italy, N-S, bid to 6♠. West for the United States, Norman Kay, led the ◇8, won by dummy's ace. Garozzo gave the hand a typically meticulous play. He led the ♣J, covered by the queen and ace, and played his other diamond toward dummy.

If West had ruffed this, declarer would only have had to guess the club position to make the slam. (Dummy would follow with a low diamond, and Garozzo would subsequently throw his heart loser on the ◇K.) However, Kay not only refused to ruff, he threw a *heart*, not his worthless fifth club, for fear of suggesting the club position to declarer.

Garozzo won dummy's ◇K and still could have made the contract with an inspired guess. In practice, he very reasonably tried a club to the nine. Kay won and alertly returned a club, killing the slam, and the United States gained 13 IMPs. (The U.S. N-S pair stopped in game.)

Problems

1. Dlr: South   ♠ 10 7 5 4 2
    Vul: N-S   ♡ Q 10 7 6
                   ◇ 9 6
                   ♣ J 2

                          ♠ J 9 3
                          ♡ 2
                          ◇ Q J 10 8 4
                          ♣ Q 9 6 3

WEST	NORTH	EAST	SOUTH
			1 ♡
Dbl	3 ♡¹	4 ♢	4 ♡
All Pass			

¹ Pre-emptive. With a good hand, North would start with a redouble, or bid 2NT to indicate a strong raise to 3♡.

West, your partner, leads a trump. Declarer wins the king and leads to the ♡Q. What do you discard?

2. Dlr: West   ♠ J 3
        Vul: None   ♡ J 5 3
                          ♢ K 8 5 2
                          ♣ A K 5 4

♠ Q 5
♡ K 7
♢ A Q J 10 7 3   □
♣ 8 7 3

WEST	NORTH	EAST	SOUTH
1 ♢	Pass	1 ♡	4 ♠
All Pass			

You, West, lead the ♡K. Partner signals high, so you continue. East cashes the ♡Q and ♡A. What do you discard?

Solutions
1.   Throw the ♢Q, warning partner not to lay down the ♢A if he has it.

```
                    ♠ 10 7 5 4 2
                    ♡ Q 10 7 6
                    ♢ 9 6
                    ♣ J 2
   ♠ A Q 8 6                        ♠ J 9 3
   ♡ 9 4                            ♡ 2
   ♢ A 7 2          □               ♢ Q J 10 8 4
   ♣ K 10 7 4                       ♣ Q 9 6 3
                    ♠ K
                    ♡ A K J 8 5 3
                    ♢ K 5 3
                    ♣ A 8 5
```

Declarer probably will lead to the ♠K at trick three. Partner will know from your discard that leading a diamond cannot gain. If he exits with a black card, the contract will be set.

2.　Discard the ◇A! Partner will have no choice but to continue with a fourth round of hearts, promoting your ♠Q for the setting trick.

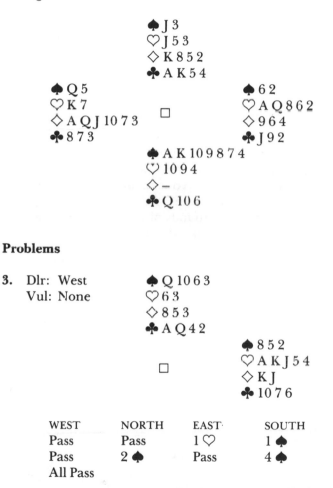

```
                    ♠ J 3
                    ♡ J 5 3
                    ◇ K 8 5 2
                    ♣ A K 5 4
  ♠ Q 5                            ♠ 6 2
  ♡ K 7                            ♡ A Q 8 6 2
  ◇ A Q J 10 7 3        □         ◇ 9 6 4
  ♣ 8 7 3                          ♣ J 9 2
                    ♠ A K 10 9 8 7 4
                    ♡ 10 9 4
                    ◇ –
                    ♣ Q 10 6
```

Problems

3.　Dlr: West　　♠ Q 10 6 3
　　Vul: None　　♡ 6 3
　　　　　　　　◇ 8 5 3
　　　　　　　　♣ A Q 4 2

　　　　　　　　　　　　　　♠ 8 5 2
　　　　　　　　　□　　　♡ A K J 5 4
　　　　　　　　　　　　　　◇ K J
　　　　　　　　　　　　　　♣ 10 7 6

WEST	NORTH	EAST	SOUTH
Pass	Pass	1 ♡	1 ♠
Pass	2 ♠	Pass	4 ♠
All Pass			

West, your partner, leads the ♡2. You win the king and ace, and declarer's queen falls. At trick three, you try a shift to the ◇K – ace, six, three. Declarer draws three rounds of trumps, partner throwing two hearts, and continues with ♣K, ♣Q and ♣A, discarding a diamond. After some thought, he leads dummy's fourth club. What do you discard?

4. Dlr: South
Vul: N-S

♠ A 8 6 4
♡ 8 7
♢ 8 7 4
♣ K Q 4 3

♠ Q 7
♡ Q 9
♢ K 10 6 5 3
♣ J 10 8 6

WEST	NORTH	EAST	SOUTH
			1 ♡
Pass	1 ♠	Pass	3 ♡
Pass	4 ♡	All Pass	

West, your partner, leads the ♠5, ducked to your queen. Declarer follows with the three. Your spade return goes to ten, jack, and ace. Now declarer leads a diamond to the queen, winning, and reels off three rounds of trumps. West following with the six, five, and ten. What do you discard on the third trump?

Solutions

3.

♠ Q 10 6 3
♡ 6 3
♢ 8 5 3
♣ A Q 4 2

♠ 7
♡ 10 8 7 2
♢ Q 9 6 2
♣ J 9 8 5

♠ 8 5 2
♡ A K J 5 4
♢ K J
♣ 10 7 6

♠ A K J 9 4
♡ Q 9
♢ A 10 7 4
♣ K 3

Jettison the ♢J. Otherwise, declarer will ruff the fourth club and exit with a diamond. West cannot profitably play his queen, and when you win the jack you have to give declarer a ruff-and-discard and his contract.

Declarer could have made his game leading a diamond after playing just three rounds of clubs; but he judged that your hand was

♠ x x x
♡ A K J x x
♢ K
♣ J 10 x x.

If you had followed to the fourth club, he would have discarded a diamond, end-playing you.

4.   Discard the ♣J, giving partner the count. This cannot cost the contract – if declarer has the ♣A, he is cold for the rest of the tricks. But if partner has the ♣A, you want him to take it at the right time. The full deal:

```
                      ♠ A 8 6 4
                      ♡ 8 7
                      ♢ 8 7 4
                      ♣ K Q 4 3
       ♠ K J 9 5                      ♠ Q 7
       ♡ 10 6 5                       ♡ Q 9
       ♢ J 9                          ♢ K 10 6 5 3
       ♣ A 9 7 2                      ♣ J 10 8 6
                      ♠ 10 3 2
                      ♡ A K J 4 3 2
                      ♢ A Q 2
                      ♣ 5
```

When declarer leads a club, partner will play the ace, cash his spade, and force declarer to ruff a spade. Declarer must lose a diamond in the end.

Quiz 17

Good Timing

Discussing good timing in an earlier book, I cited Hugh Kelsey's sage comment that declarer can find himself blessed with ample high cards, yet fail if he plays them in the wrong order. This admonition is even truer in defensive play, where one pair must struggle along with the worst part of the high-card strength and fewer opportunities to lead.

The following situation was mentioned in Quiz 13, but it is important enough to repeat.

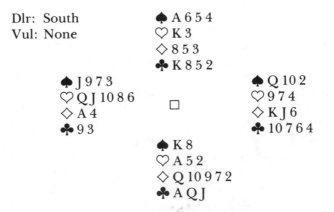

Dlr: South
Vul: None

```
                    ♠ A 6 5 4
                    ♡ K 3
                    ◇ 8 5 3
                    ♣ K 8 5 2
    ♠ J 9 7 3                      ♠ Q 10 2
    ♡ Q J 10 8 6        □          ♡ 9 7 4
    ◇ A 4                          ◇ K J 6
    ♣ 9 3                          ♣ 10 7 6 4
                    ♠ K 8
                    ♡ A 5 2
                    ◇ Q 10 9 7 2
                    ♣ A Q J
```

South opens 1 NT. North tries Stayman and then signs off in 3 NT. West leads the ♡Q. Declarer ducks the first heart, wins the second with dummy's king, and leads a low diamond. If East is well versed in the principles of no-trump defence, he will put up the ◇K and return his last heart. This play can lose nothing, since declarer is about to take a successful finesse if he has the ◇AQ. It is vital to get the defensive timing right by preserving West's entry to the hearts.

That is a textbook situation, but other instances of defensive timing are more taxing. The next deal would be too difficult for most West players.

144

```
Dlr: South          ♠ Q J 10 4
Vul: N-S            ♡ 5 3
                    ◇ Q 6 5 3
                    ♣ A J 8
    ♠ K 9 8 5                       ♠ A 7 3
    ♡ 9 6                           ♡ K Q 10 8 4 2
    ◇ A 10 9 8      □               ◇ 7 2
    ♣ 7 4 2                         ♣ 6 3
                    ♠ 6 2
                    ♡ A J 7
                    ◇ K J 4
                    ♣ K Q 10 9 5
```

WEST	NORTH	EAST	SOUTH
			1 ♣
Pass	1 ♠	2 ♡	Pass
Pass	3 ♣	Pass	3 NT
All Pass			

After N-S struggle into 3 NT, West leads the ♡9 to the queen and ace. Declarer crosses to the ♣J and leads a diamond to the seven and king. West thinks that declarer is likely to have the ◇J, too. He makes the fine play of ducking, and declarer is finished. If declarer leads another diamond, the defence can take two diamonds, two hearts, and a spade; and no other play by declarer offers any hope.

Note that if West wins the first diamond, he can do nothing to keep declarer from taking nine tricks. (Declarer, of course, mistimed *his* play – he was safe for the contract by ducking the first trick.)

Another area of defensive timing involves combining chances. Often, a defender will have two or more possible lines of play. Sometimes it won't matter in which order he tries them. On other occasions, he must take care to start with the line that will not irrevocably give away the contract if it fails.

Dlr: North   ♠ K J 10 4 3
Vul: Both   ♡ Q 9 6 2
                    ◇ 6 5 3
                    ♣ K

♠ 8 7 5 2   ♠ A 9
♡ A 5   ♡ 8 4
◇ A K   □   ◇ J 10 9 7 2
♣ J 10 9 4 2   ♣ 8 7 6 5

                    ♠ Q 6
                    ♡ K J 10 7 3
                    ◇ Q 8 4
                    ♣ A Q 3

WEST	NORTH	EAST	SOUTH
	Pass	Pass	1 ♡
Pass	3 ♡	All Pass	

West leads the ◇K and ◇A (suggesting a doubleton). In an expert game, East would follow with the jack on the second round, as a suit-preference signal for spades. But West should lead a spade regardless. Clearly, East must hold an ace to beat the contract. A spade switch can't cost if declarer has the ace; but if declarer has the ♣A and the queen, a club switch will allow him to discard dummy's remaining diamond, avoiding the impending ruff.

I was West on the following deal from a recent club duplicate game.

Dlr: North   ♠ A Q J 6 4
Vul: E-W   ♡ Q 9
Matchpoints   ◇ A 6 5
                    ♣ Q 10 3

♠ 7 5 2   ♠ K 10 8 3
♡ A 10 7 6 3   ♡ 8 5 4
◇ 8 3   □   ◇ 9 7
♣ K 5 2   ♣ A J 8 4

                    ♠ 9
                    ♡ K J 2
                    ◇ K Q J 10 4 2
                    ♣ 9 7 6

WEST	NORTH	EAST	SOUTH
	1 ♠	Pass	2 ◇
Pass	2 ♠	Pass	2 NT
Pass	3 NT	All Pass	

I led a heart, won by dummy's nine. Declarer, for reasons best known to him, cashed the ◇A and played a diamond to the jack before leading a second heart. Partner had petered in diamonds, so I knew declarer had nine tricks to take. I grabbed the ♡A and switched to a low club, and we took four tricks in the suit to put the contract down one.

Later I realized that I had misdefended. If declarer had held the ♣J instead of East, my defence would have given away an overtrick. I should have started by leading the ♣K. If partner lacked the ♣J, he would signal low, and I could switch to a spade to hold declarer to just nine tricks.

On other hands, the defenders' aim is not to retain their own options but rather to keep declarer from exercising all of his. This is a deal from the 1977 Bermuda Bowl.

Dlr: North   ♠ 7 2
Vul: N-S   ♡ K Q J 7 4 3
                ◇ A 9
                ♣ J 6 4

♠ 8 4   ♠ 10 6 5 3
♡ 10 9 5 2   ♡ A 8
◇ Q J 10 8 2   □   ◇ 5 4 3
♣ 10 2   ♣ K 8 5 3

                ♠ A K Q J 9
                ♡ 6
                ◇ K 7 6
                ♣ A Q 9 7

At one table in the United States–Taiwan match, John Swanson and Paul Soloway bid 6♠ for the United States and went down one. The Taiwanese N-S pair in the other room also reached the slam:

WEST	NORTH	EAST	SOUTH
Kantar	*Lin*	*Eisenberg*	*Tai*
	1 ♡	Pass	1 ♠
Pass	2 ♡	Pass	3 ♣
Pass	3 ♡	Pass	4 ◇
Pass	4 ♠	Pass	4 NT
Pass	5 ◇	Pass	6 ♠
All Pass			

Eddie Kantar led the ◇Q. Declarer won with the king, drew trumps, discarding a club and a heart from dummy, and led a heart to the king and ace. Billy Eisenberg returned a diamond to dummy's ace. Hearts failed to split, but declarer continued by leading ♣J. With the lucky fall of the ♣10, the slam was home. Seventeen IMPs to Taiwan.

It might have been a different story had East returned the ♣8 when he won the ♡A. South would then have had to guess whether to stake the contract on a 3-3 heart split or finesse in clubs.

The idea of removing declarer's options can even be extended to the opening lead. Several years ago, in a team event, I held as South:

♠ 10 6 4
♡ 10 8 6 5 3
◇ 7 6 4
♣ K 9

WEST	EAST
	1 ♡
2 ♣	4 ♡
4 NT	5 ◇
6 ♡	

I led the ♣9 initially, reasoning that declarer would never finesse at trick one, running the risk of a ruff, when the hearts would look solid to him. So we would take a trump trick and a surprise trick in clubs.

The story had an ironic ending. The full deal was:

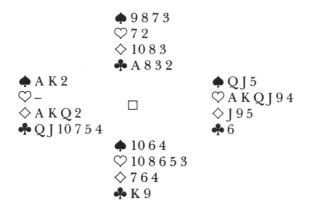

♠ 9 8 7 3
♡ 7 2
◇ 10 8 3
♣ A 8 3 2

♠ A K 2　　　　　　　♠ Q J 5
♡ –　　　　　　　　　♡ A K Q J 9 4
◇ A K Q 2　　□　　　◇ J 9 5
♣ Q J 10 7 5 4　　　　♣ 6

♠ 10 6 4
♡ 10 8 6 5 3
◇ 7 6 4
♣ K 9

Sure enough, a club was the only lead to beat the slam.

Problems

1. Dlr: South　　♠ Q 6
　 Vul: None　　　♡ J 7 6 5
　　　　　　　　　◇ A J 10 7 3
　　　　　　　　　♣ 7 6

　　　　　　　　　　　　　♠ J 10 9 8
　　　　　　　　□　　　　♡ K 8 3
　　　　　　　　　　　　　◇ K Q 9
　　　　　　　　　　　　　♣ Q 10 3

WEST	NORTH	EAST	SOUTH
			1 NT
Pass	2 ♣	Pass	2 ♠
Pass	2 NT	Pass	3 NT
All Pass			

West, your partner, leads the ♣5. Declarer ducks your queen, ducks again when you return the ♣10, and takes his ace on the third club. The ◇2 is led to the six and ten. How do you defend?

2. Dlr: East
     Vul: None

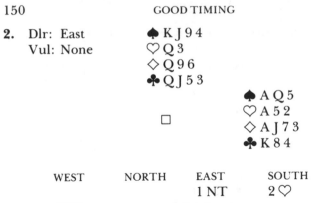

♠ K J 9 4
♡ Q 3
◇ Q 9 6
♣ Q J 5 3

                              ♠ A Q 5
                              ♡ A 5 2
            □   ◇ A J 7 3
                              ♣ K 8 4

WEST	NORTH	EAST	SOUTH
		1 NT	2 ♡

All Pass

West, your partner, leads an inspired ◇K and continues with the ◇2 to your jack. How do you continue?

Solutions

1.
                    ♠ Q 6
                    ♡ J 7 6 5
                    ◇ A J 10 7 3
                    ♣ 7 6
♠ 7 5 2   ♠ J 10 9 8
♡ 10 4 2   ♡ K 8 3
◇ 6 5   □   ◇ K Q 9
♣ K J 9 5 2   ♣ Q 10 3
                    ♠ A K 4 3
                    ♡ A Q 9
                    ◇ 8 4 2
                    ♣ A 8 4

Win the ◇K and return the ♡8, forcing declarer to choose prematurely between the heart finesse and another diamond finesse. If he goes up with the ♡A and tries a diamond to the jack, you will have to try to avoid looking smug as you cash the ♡K.

If you return the ♠J, declarer will win the queen and king, and finesse again in diamonds. When he learns that only three diamond tricks are available, he will have no choice but to take the heart finesse.

2. Return a *low* diamond for partner to ruff. He will lead a trump, and you play ace and another. Declarer can win in dummy and finesse in clubs, but he still must lose a spade and another diamond for down one.

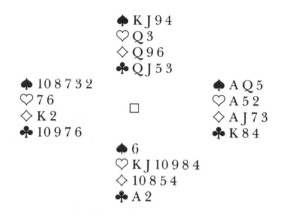

```
                  ♠ K J 9 4
                  ♡ Q 3
                  ◇ Q 9 6
                  ♣ Q J 5 3
  ♠ 10 8 7 3 2                    ♠ A Q 5
  ♡ 7 6              □            ♡ A 5 2
  ◇ K 2                           ◇ A J 7 3
  ♣ 10 9 7 6                      ♣ K 8 4
                  ♠ 6
                  ♡ K J 10 9 8 4
                  ◇ 10 8 5 4
                  ♣ A 2
```

If you cash your ◇A at trick three, the contract will be made – depending on your next play, declarer will either score his ◇10 or ruff it in dummy for the eighth trick.

Problems

3. Dlr: South
    Vul: N-S

```
                  ♠ Q J 3
                  ♡ K 4
                  ◇ 9 6 5
                  ♣ K Q J 5 4
  ♠ K 5
  ♡ Q 10 9 5         □
  ◇ A Q 10 2
  ♣ 10 8 7
```

WEST	NORTH	EAST	SOUTH
			1 ♠
Pass	2 ♣	Pass	2 ◇
Pass	3 ♠	Pass	4 ♠
All Pass			

You, West, lead the ♡10. Dummy's king wins, East playing the two and declarer the three. The ♣Q is then led and run to your king. What do you lead now?

4. Dlr: South   ♠ A 10 7 4 3
     Vul: E-W   ♡ 9 6 3
                ◇ 10 9 6 5
                ♣ A

♠ K J 8
♡ K 10 7 5   □
◇ 7
♣ 10 9 8 7 5

WEST	NORTH	EAST	SOUTH
			1 ♣
Pass	1 ♠	Pass	3 ♣
Pass	3 ◇	Pass	3 NT
All Pass			

You, West, lead the ♡5, and East's jack loses to declarer's queen. Declarer goes to the ♣A, East following low, and plays a spade to the two and queen. Do you win this trick? If so, what do you return?

Solutions

3. You must play East for either the ♣A or the ◇K. If you lead a club and declarer turns up with the ace, you get to watch him cash eleven tricks. Keep your options open by leading the ◇2.

                ♠ Q J 3
                ♡ K 4
                ◇ 9 6 5
                ♣ K Q J 5 4

♠ K 5   ♠ 8 6 2
♡ Q 10 9 5   □   ♡ J 8 7 6 2
◇ A Q 10 2   ◇ K 7
♣ 10 8 7   ♣ 9 6 3

                ♠ A 10 9 7 4
                ♡ A 3
                ◇ J 8 4 3
                ♣ A 2

You are still all right if declarer holds

♠ A 10 9 x x
♡ A x
◇ K J x x
♣ x x

or even

♠ A 10 9 x x
♡ A x
◇ K J x x x
♣ x

4.

♠ A 10 7 4 3
♡ 9 6 3
◇ 10 9 6 5
♣ A

♠ K J 8   ♠ 9 6 2
♡ K 10 7 5   ♡ J 8 2
◇ 7   □   ◇ A K J 8 3 2
♣ 10 9 8 7 5   ♣ 4

♠ Q 5
♡ A Q 4
◇ Q 4
♣ K Q J 6 3 2

The deal is from the 1970 Bermuda Bowl. The play to the first three tricks was the same at both tables. At one table, West returned the ♡K at trick four. The U.S. declarer, Bobby Wolff, won and cashed the ♣K. When clubs unexpectedly split 5-1, Wolff took two more rounds and then tried a spade to the ten. The spade position was as favourable as the clubs had been foul, and Wolff scored his game.

At the other table, Bob Hamman was West for the United States. After winning the ♠K, Hamman alertly returned a *spade*. Of course, the Italian declarer went up with the ace, planning to run his clubs. At this stage, he had no inkling that the suit was 5-1, and Hamman gave him no chance to find out and then fall back on the spade suit. The outcome – down two, 11 IMPs to the United States.

Quiz 18

Card Combinations We Have Known

The proper handling of card combinations is at the heart of good declarer play, but there are many standard *defensive* card combinations as well. In fact, this is probably a more difficult area for the defenders to master. Declarer, at least, has all his resources in plain view, but playing good defence requires imagination and a developed sense of the cards.

The defenders customarily lead the highest card in a sequence to force out declarer's top cards and promote their own intermediates. Even if a defender's holding is not truly a sequence, similar results may be achieved. The position below requires West to make an honour-trapping play (often called a 'surrounding' play).

Q 7 3

K J 9   □   A 6 4 2

10 8 5

West, deducing that his partner has the ace, leads this suit. The proper card to lead is the *jack*, which makes use of the nine as though it were the ten. Note that this play leaves declarer helpless, while no other attack by West would be sure to succeed.

♠ K 5
♡ Q 10 7
♢ J 7 4
♣ A Q 10 7 5

♠ 10 9 8 4   ♠ Q J 3 2
♡ K 5   ♡ 8 6 3
♢ K 10 8 3   □   ♢ Q 6 5
♣ 9 8 3   ♣ K 6 2

♠ A 7 6
♡ A J 9 4 2
♢ A 9 2
♣ J 4

South becomes declarer in 4♡. West leads the ♠10. Declarer wins in dummy and finesses the ♡10 to West's king. Looking at dummy's strong clubs, West should be anxious to switch to a diamond. But not just any diamond will do – West must play the *ten*, the card he would lead if he had a sequence headed by that card. If West leads a low card instead and declarer plays low from dummy, the defence is ruined.

In a pinch, the defenders may have to try for a surrounding play in precarious circumstances:

$$\begin{array}{ccc} & J\,6\,3 & \\ K\,10\,4 & \square & Q\,8\,7\,2 \\ & A\,9\,5 & \end{array}$$

West, who must break this suit, does best to lead the *ten*. Luckily, East holds the eight and seven as well as the queen.

Defenders who frequently try honour-trapping plays may risk becoming trapped themselves. They constantly must try to count declarer's distribution so disasters like the one below can be avoided:

$$\begin{array}{ccc} & 10\,6\,4 & \\ A\,7\,5\,2 & \square & K\,J\,8\,3 \\ & Q\,9 & \end{array}$$

East must lead this suit and proudly attempts an honour-trapping play by starting with the jack. Not a roaring success.

Another problem the defenders must contend with is a blocked suit. In Quiz 4 we saw a couple of unblocking examples. Here is another:

$$\begin{array}{ccc} & Q\,7 & \\ A\,10\,8\,6\,5\,2 & \square & J\,9 \\ & K\,4\,3 & \end{array}$$

West leads the six of this suit against no-trump. When declarer plays dummy's queen, East must jettison the jack.

A more difficult illustration of the same idea:

Dlr: North
Vul: N-S

♠ K 8 6 2
♡ A 8
♢ K Q 9 6
♣ Q 6 5

♠ 10 7 4
♡ J 10 9 5
♢ J 8 3
♣ A K 2

☐

♠ J 9 5 3
♡ 7 6 3
♢ A 10 7 2
♣ 8 3

♠ A Q
♡ K Q 4 2
♢ 5 4
♣ J 10 9 7 4

WEST	NORTH	EAST	SOUTH
	1 ♢	Pass	1 ♡
Pass	1 ♠	Pass	2 NT
Pass	3 NT	All Pass	

South plays in 3 NT. He wins the ♡J opening lead in dummy and leads a club to the jack and king. To give the defence a chance now, West must shift to the ♢8.

Problems

1. Dlr: South
    Vul:

♠ K 9 3 2
♡ 9
♢ A Q 7 6 4
♣ Q 5 4

☐

♠ 10 8 6 5
♡ A J 7 4
♢ 9 8 5
♣ K 2

WEST	NORTH	EAST	SOUTH
			1 NT
Pass	2 ♣	Pass	2 ♢
Pass	3 NT	All Pass	

West, your partner, leads the ♡3. Plan your defence.

2. Dlr: East   ♠ J 7 3
    Vul: Both   ♡ J 10 9
                        ◇ A Q 10 3
                        ♣ A 8 4

♠ A 10 8 6
♡ A 2
◇ 2   □
♣ Q J 7 6 3 2

WEST	NORTH	EAST	SOUTH
		Pass	Pass
1 ♣	Pass	Pass	1 NT[1]
Pass	3 NT	All Pass	

[1] in the balancing seat, 12-14 HCP

You, West, lead a hopeful ♣6. East can only contribute the five, and declarer wins the ten. At trick two, declarer leads a low heart. How do you defend?

Solutions

1. Win the ♡A and return the ♡7 or ♡J. You may need to hang on to that precious ♡4 until the fourth round of the suit. The full deal:

                    ♠ K 9 3 2
                    ♡ 9
                    ◇ A Q 7 6 4
                    ♣ Q 5 4
♠ Q 7   ♠ 10 8 6 5
♡ K 10 6 3 2   ♡ A J 7 4
◇ 10 3   □   ◇ 9 8 5
♣ 9 8 7 6   ♣ K 2
                    ♠ A J 4
                    ♡ Q 8 5
                    ◇ K J 2
                    ♣ A J 10 3

If East returns the ♡4 at trick two and declarer plays the eight, the suit will block and the defence can manage only four heart tricks before giving up the lead. Declarer then takes the rest.

N-S's bidding was not best, but it will cost them nothing unless East is alert.

2. It isn't often that you know *exactly* how many HCP your partner has at trick one. East probably has a red king and the ♠Q. If he had, say, the ♡Q and ♠K, declarer would go to dummy and lead the ♡J for a finesse.

If you beat this hand, it will be with the spade suit. Go in with the ♡A and shift to the ♠*10*, an honour-trapping play. The full deal:

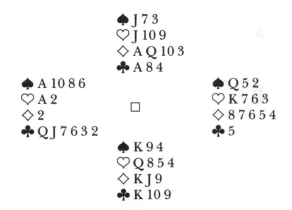

```
                ♠ J 7 3
                ♡ J 10 9
                ◇ A Q 10 3
                ♣ A 8 4
♠ A 10 8 6                      ♠ Q 5 2
♡ A 2                           ♡ K 7 6 3
◇ 2              □              ◇ 8 7 6 5 4
♣ Q J 7 6 3 2                   ♣ 5
                ♠ K 9 4
                ♡ Q 8 5 4
                ◇ K J 9
                ♣ K 10 9
```

Note that *you must win the first heart.* If East wins, he cannot attack spades effectively from his side. And if you play low and East ducks as well, declarer has nine tricks (counting one he'll take in spades or a second heart).

Your opening lead didn't look too dynamic, but it was better than a low spade.

Problems

3.   Dlr: South   ♠ Q 4
        Vul: None   ♡ K Q J 6 3
                            ◇ Q 10
                            ♣ K 8 6 4

    ♠ J 10 9 8
    ♡ 10 4 2   □
    ◇ K J 7 4
    ♣ A 5

WEST	NORTH	EAST	SOUTH
			1 ◇
Pass	1 ♡	Pass	1 ♠
Pass	2 ♣	Pass	2 NT
Pass	3 NT	All Pass	

You, West, lead ♠J, and dummy's queen holds. At trick two, declarer plays a club to the two, queen and your ace. How do you continue?

4.   Dlr: South   ♠ Q 9 6 3
        Vul: Both   ♡ K 7 4
                         ◇ K Q 5
                         ♣ K 7 2

                                   ♠ 8 2
                                   ♡ 10 8 6
                         ☐   ◇ A 9 6 2
                                   ♣ Q J 8 3

WEST	NORTH	EAST	SOUTH
			1 ♠
Pass	3 ♠	Pass	4 ♠
All Pass			

West, your partner, leads the ◇J. You capture dummy's king with the ace and return the ◇2. Declarer wins in dummy, ruffs a diamond, and draws two rounds of trumps with the ace and king. Now the ♣A and ♣K are cashed, and declarer exits with a club to your jack, partner following suit. How do you defend?

Solutions

3.   Declarer probably has the ♡A, else he would have started on hearts immediately instead of clubs. In that case, you can count nine tricks for him – five hearts, three spades, and a club. So you must switch to diamonds despite declarer's opening bid. Partner will have to hold the ◇A, but you still must lead the king to make sure the defensive timing is right. The full deal:

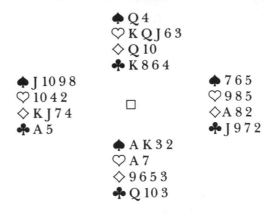

On the ♢K, East will unblock the eight. Then a diamond to the ace and a diamond back through the 9-6 to your J-7 will get the job done.

4.

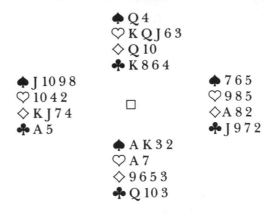

You are end-played and obliged to open up hearts. As usual, be alert for 'surrounding' possibilities. This time, the lead of the *eight* works. Some of these honour-trapping plays are pretty obscure, aren't they?

If you lead the ten, declarer covers with the queen – West is fixed whether he wins or ducks. If you lead low, partner has to put up the jack to force dummy's king, and declarer can lead low to the nine next to drive out the ace. Only the lead of the eight leaves declarer without recourse.

Problems

5. Dlr: South
Vul: N-S

♠ A 7
♡ Q J 8 3
◇ K 9 8 3
♣ K 10 6

☐

♠ 8 5 2
♡ 9 4 2
◇ Q 7 4
♣ A Q J 2

WEST	NORTH	EAST	SOUTH
			1 ♣
Pass	1 ♡	Pass	1 NT
Pass	3 NT	All Pass	

West, your partner, leads the ♠J. Declarer plays low from dummy and wins the queen in hand. At trick two, the ◇J is run to your queen. How do you continue?

6. Dlr: South
Vul: E-W

♠ 9 5 2
♡ 10 7
◇ A 4
♣ K Q 10 9 4 3

☐

♠ K 10 8 6
♡ A J 2
◇ K 9 8
♣ 7 6 2

WEST	NORTH	EAST	SOUTH
			1 NT
Pass	3 NT	All Pass	

West, your partner, leads the ♡9. Dummy's ten covers. Plan your defence.

Solutions

5. A spade continuation is futile. If West's spades are K-J-10-x-x, declarer must have the ◇A and the ♡A and ♡K for nine tricks in all. You must switch, but the right answer, for some reason, is hard to spot. With dummy holding just three clubs, it is sufficient to return the ♣2. Declarer may win cheaply, but your three honours remain poised behind the king, and you are worth three tricks if partner has a red-suit entry. The full deal:

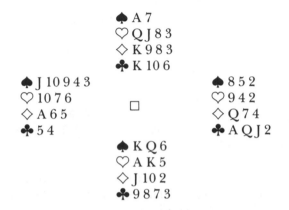

♠ A 7
♡ Q J 8 3
◇ K 9 8 3
♣ K 10 6

♠ J 10 9 4 3   ♠ 8 5 2
♡ 10 7 6   ♡ 9 4 2
◇ A 6 5   ◇ Q 7 4
♣ 5 4   ♣ A Q J 2

♠ K Q 6
♡ A K 5
◇ J 10 2
♣ 9 8 7 3

You give the contract away if you lead a club honour or any other suit at trick three.

6.

♠ 9 5 2
♡ 10 7
◇ A 4
♣ K Q 10 9 4 3

♠ A 7 4 3   ♠ K 10 8 6
♡ 9 8 6 5 3   ♡ A J 2
◇ 10 7 6   ◇ K 9 8
♣ 5   ♣ 7 6 2

♠ Q J
♡ K Q 4
◇ Q J 5 3 2
♣ A J 8

If you won the ♡A and shifted to the ♠10 to trap dummy's nine, sorry – I double-crossed you. You must lead a low spade this time and collect your four spade tricks.

West has at most 4 HCP, and there is just no chance to beat the contract unless he has the ♠A. If West has, say, the ♠Q and ◇Q, declarer has six club tricks, one diamond, two hearts, and a spade. The only alternative defence that appeals at all is a switch to the $\diamond$K, trying to kill dummy if partner has the $\clubsuit$A. But that would leave declarer with something like

$\spadesuit$ A Q J
$\heartsuit$ K Q x x
$\diamond$ Q J x x
$\clubsuit$ J x

and if he holds that hand, he can make the contract without the clubs.

Trying for an honour-trapping play is wrong here because you need *four fast spade tricks* to beat the contract.

Quiz 19

One Suit at a Time

This quiz deals with an important defensive skill. Good bridge players possess something called 'card sense', which gives them a natural advantage in drawing inferences. Luckily, card sense *can* be learned – so don't despair if you think you were missing when they doled it out.

Inferring the lie of an individual suit based on the play of that suit is a first step in the defenders' all-important task of reconstructing declarer's whole hand. The key to deduction is to put yourself in declarer's place and consider how you would have played with various holdings. In many situations, the answer will be obvious:

K 4

2 led >>>   ☐   A Q 8 5

You are defending 4♠, dummy has plenty of trumps, and this is a side suit. Partner's opening lead is the two; declarer puts up the king. Who has the jack? Clearly, partner has it – otherwise declarer would have played low from dummy, hoping West led from the queen.

It may not always be so clear what's going on. Here, for example, if declarer played low from dummy, you wouldn't be a hundred per cent sure who had the jack. Expecting you to hold the ace, declarer might well play low from dummy whatever was his holding.

♠ 10

♠ K 9   ☐

The contract is 4♠, and dummy has no entries. Declarer, who bid spades vigorously, wins the opening lead, cashes the ace of trumps, and leads the queen to your king, partner following low both times. If declarer's trumps were A-Q-J-x-x-x-x, he would start by leading low to the ten. Playing the ace first could gain nothing; even if the king fell singleton, a trick still would have to be lost to the nine. And laying down the ace first would cost a trick if either defender had K-9-x-x. So you can place declarer with an *eight*-card trump suit.

More inferences are available if you're defending a no-trump contract. A simple example:

```
              A J 9 3
    Q 5 2       □
```

Declarer attacks this suit by leading low to the nine, losing to partner's ten. Obviously, partner has the king also – declarer's play would make little sense otherwise.

```
              9 8 5 4
    K Q J 3     □
```

You lead the king – four, two, six. Partner must have either the ace or the ten. If declarer held both, he could have ensured a second stopper by winning your lead.

```
              A Q 10
    7 5 3       □
```

Declarer leads low to the ten, losing to partner's jack. Partner is very likely to have the king, too.

```
              K 5
  2 led>>>      □          A Q 7 3
```

Declarer plays low from dummy, and you win the queen. If declarer's holding were x-x-x or even 10-x-x, he would have tried dummy's king immediately. You'd expect him to have J-x-x.

Deducing single-suit holdings will help you develop your card sense, but here we must sound a warning: it can be dangerous to consider a suit outside the context of the whole hand. Here are a couple of full deals on which a defender's assessment of a single suit is the key to the best defence.

                    ♠ A 8 2
                    ♡ A K Q 9 3
                    ◇ 6 4
                    ♣ 6 5 4

♠ K 10 7 5 3   ♠ Q 4
♡ J 5   ♡ 10 8 7 6
◇ Q 10 8 7   □   ◇ K 9 2
♣ J 3   ♣ 10 9 8 7

                    ♠ J 9 6
                    ♡ 4 2
                    ◇ A J 5 3
                    ♣ A K Q 2

WEST	NORTH	EAST	SOUTH
			1 ♣
Pass	1 ♡	Pass	1 NT
Pass	3 NT	All Pass	

West leads the ♠5. If declarer were to play dummy's ace, hoping to block the suit, East could infer that declarer did not have K-J-x or J-10-x, and probably not K-10-x. He could safely unblock the queen.

This time, however, declarer ducks the first spade and wins the second round. Now he must develop four heart tricks without letting West regain the lead, so he comes to hand with a high club and leads a heart. West can infer that declarer has only two hearts, else he would have cashed a top honour in dummy first (or he might even have played off all three top honours). So West inserts the ♡J, ruining South's plan to duck a heart safely to East.

Dlr: North   ♠ A K 10 6 5 3
Vul: Both   ♡ 7 3
                          ◇ 6
                          ♣ K 7 5 3

♠ J 9 4   ♠ Q 8
♡ 4 2   ♡ J 9 8
◇ J 9 7 4   □   ◇ A K 10 2
♣ Q 8 4 2   ♣ A J 9 6

                          ♠ 7 2
                          ♡ A K Q 10 6 5
                          ◇ Q 8 5 3
                          ♣ 10

WEST	NORTH	EAST	SOUTH
	1 ♠	Dbl	2 ♡
Pass	2 ♠	Pass	4 ♡
All Pass			

West leads the ♢4 to East's king, declarer playing the five. Declarer wins the trump switch and plays a spade to the four, ten, and queen. What should East return?

East has a good picture of declarer's hand. South has at least three diamonds and should have exactly two spades to play the suit in this manner. If he had a solid seven-card trump suit, he would have ruffed a diamond for the contract – so he must have only six hearts. Since declarer did not choose to take a diamond ruff, he must have thought it wouldn't help him take ten tricks.* He must be relying on the spades, so East must return a spade, cutting declarer's link with dummy.

* The play would be interesting if declarer ruffed a diamond at trick three and led a club. To beat the contract, West would have to win and lead a spade. On any other defence, East falls victim to a three-suit squeeze. Do you see how declarer can always make the contract?

Problems (A)

You are defending a *suit contract*. (To make things as simple as possible, assume that the suits below are side suits, dummy has plenty of trumps, and both declarer and dummy have ample entries.)

1.   K J 3
    2 led>>>   ☐   Q 9 4

The two is the opening lead. Declarer plays low from dummy. Which card do you play?

2.   K J 9 3
        A 6 5   ☐

Declarer leads low to the nine, losing to partner's ten. Who has the queen? How many cards does declarer have?

3.   A 8 6 2
                            ☐   K J 9

Declarer leads low from his hand and ducks in dummy. Who has the queen?

4.   K 10 9 4
       A 6 5   ☐

Declarer leads low to dummy's nine, losing to partner's jack. Could declarer have Q-x? Q-x-x? x-x-x? x-x?

5.   A 10 5
       2 led>>>   ☐   Q 9 7

The two is the opening lead. Declarer plays the ten. Who has the jack? Who has the eight?

6.   Q J 10 3
       K 9 5 4   ☐

Declarer leads low toward dummy. Who has the ace?

7.   10 5 3
       K Q 9 4   ☐

You lead the king, which holds. Could declarer have the ace? The jack? The ace-jack?

8.   A J 4
       2 led>>>   ☐   10 8 6

The two is the opening lead, and dummy plays the jack. Who has the king? Who has the queen? Suppose declarer plays the ace. Now who has the king? The queen?

9.   A 7 3
       K 8 5 2   ☐

Your opening lead is the two and declarer wins the ace. Who has the queen?

10.   A Q 3
        K 9 7 5 2   ☐

Your opening lead is the five, and dummy's ace wins. What is declarer's most likely holding?

Solutions (A)

(The following inferences generally are sound. However, we repeat our admonition about always considering individual suits within the context of the whole hand. When declarer is able to place the cards, or perhaps for tactical reasons, he may depart from the normal way of attacking a suit.)

1.   Play the nine, since partners seldom underlead aces against suit contracts – not at trick one, anyway.

2.   Partner has the queen. Declarer is likely to have three (or four) cards – if he had one or two, he would have tried the jack or king on the first round.

3.   Partner has the queen. If declarer had Q-x or Q-x-x, he would have led toward the queen.

4.   Declarer could have queen doubleton or tripleton but is more likely to have three small cards from his failure to play to a high honour before finessing. He is not likely to have two small, else he usually would have gone up with dummy's king, hoping for just one loser in the suit.

5.   Partner probably has the jack (but declarer could be playing deceptively or trying to get an entry to dummy). If partner has the jack, he should have the eight also – if declarer had K-8-x, his percentage play would be low from dummy.

6.   Partner has the ace (unless declarer somehow knows you have the king and he is trying to sneak a trick by you).

7.   Declarer might have the ace or the jack, but he can hardly have both cards – in that case, ducking would cost a trick.

8.   Declarer is marked with one honour (partner would not lead low from the king and queen). If declarer had the queen, he would duck the opening lead. When he plays the jack, he must hold the king. If declarer plays the ace, he must hold the king *and* queen for his play to make sense.

9. Partner should have the queen, judging from declarer's refusal to let the opening lead run to his hand. However, if some fast discards are available in dummy, declarer might proceed to win the first trick, planning to throw his queen away.

10. Declarer probably has a singleton. Again, though, he could have his reasons for going up even without a singleton. He could be planning to discard his losers in this suit, or he might need to win the first trick to gain a *tempo*.

Problems (B)

You are defending a no-trump contract. Again, assume that declarer has adequate entries in both hands.

11.   J 4
    3 led>>>   □   K 9 5 2

Partner's opening lead is the three – four, king, ace. Did declarer start with A-Q-x? A-x-x? A-10-x?

12.   Q 8
    4 led>>>   □   K 10 6 3

Partner's opening lead is the four, dummy plays the eight. Does declarer have A-x-x? A-J-x?

13.   Q 10 8 6 3
                   □   K 7 5

Declarer wins the first trick in his hand, goes to dummy with another suit, and leads the three of this, a third suit. Who has the ace?

14.   A Q 4
    K 10 7 5 2   □

Your opening lead is the five; dummy's queen wins. Who has the jack?

15.   A 8 5 3

□   K 6 2

Declarer leads low from dummy. Can declarer have Q-J-10-x?
J-10-9-x? Q-J-9-x? Q-10-x? J-9-x-x? J-10-x-x?

16.   Q 10 8 3
A K 5 2   □

Declarer leads low; you duck, and dummy's eight loses to
partner's nine. Who has the jack?

17.   Q 3
J 9 5 2   □

Your opening lead is the two, and dummy's queen is covered by
the king and ace. Can declarer have A-10-x? A-10? A-x-x? A-x?

18.   A J 6 2

□   K 8 5 3

Declarer leads low from dummy. Can declarer have Q-10-x?
Q-x? Q-9-x?

19.   A 10 7
4 led>>>   □   K Q 5

Partner leads the four; declarer puts up dummy's ace. Who has
the jack?

20.   A K 7
6 led>>>   □   Q 4

Partner leads the six; declarer wins an honour in dummy. Who
has the jack?

Solutions (B)

11. If declarer had either A-Q-x or A-x-x, he would have
played dummy's jack to the first trick, hoping it would hold.
A-10-x is his most likely holding.

12. Declarer would have put up the queen holding either A-x-x or A-J-x, hoping it would hold. You should play the king in case declarer's holding is J-x.

13. Unless declarer is playing a very deep game, partner has the ace. Why would declarer go to dummy just to lead to the ace?

14. Partner has the jack, else declarer would have played low from dummy.

15. Declarer would finesse with Q-J-10-x or Q-J-9-x, and double finesse with J-10-9-x. The other three holdings are entirely possible, and in all three cases you need to play low. (It would be equally correct to·play low if your holding was K-x.)

16. Partner has the jack.

17. With A-10-x, declarer would have ducked in dummy to ensure two tricks. A-x or A-x-x is probable, A-10 possible.

18. Declarer cannot have Q-10-x, with which he would have finessed. With Q-9-x, he might have preferred to play the ace first, then a low one. Q-x is the most probable holding.

19. Partner is likely to have the jack, and you should consider unblocking an honour. If declarer had J-x-(x), from his point of view he might get two tricks by ducking, setting up a later finesse.

20. According to the Rule of Eleven, declarer has just one card higher than the six. The odds are against its being the jack, but if it were, declarer might have taken his only chance to make a third trick by ducking the opening lead. If your entry situation permits it, you should consider unblocking your queen.

Problems (C)

21. Dlr: South   ♠ Q 10 5
    Vul: Both   ♡ K J 10 6 4
                 ◇ A 8 5
                 ♣ 10 5

   ♠ 7 4
   ♡ A 5
   ◇ K 10 9 6 2   ☐
   ♣ A J 8 3

WEST	NORTH	EAST	SOUTH
			1 ♠
Pass	2 ♡	Pass	2 ♠
Pass	3 ♣	Pass	4 ♠
All Pass			

You, West, lead the ◇10. Dummy's ace wins, partner playing the four and declarer the seven. Declarer draws two rounds of trumps with the ace and jack. East following low-high. Next, declarer leads the ♡Q, and you take your ace. How do you continue?

22. Dlr: West   ♠ Q 7 5 2
    Vul: None   ♡ A 10 7 5
                 ◇ Q 10 6
                 ♣ 7 5

   ♠ A 10 6
   ♡ 9 3
   ◇ K 7 5 4 2   ☐
   ♣ Q J 4

WEST	NORTH	EAST	SOUTH
Pass	Pass	1 ♠	2 ♡
3 ♠	4 ♡	All Pass	

You, West, lead the ♠A and continue with the ten. Declarer ruffs the second spade, leads a heart to the ace, and plays a club to the two, ten, and your jack. How do you continue?

23. Dlr: East   ♠ K 8 5 3 2
         Vul: N-S   ♡ A 8 5 3 2
                          ◇ 8 6
                          ♣ K

♠ A 7
♡ 4
◇ Q J 9 5 2   □
♣ 9 8 7 6 3

WEST	NORTH	EAST	SOUTH
		Pass	1 ♣
Pass	1 NT	Pass	2 ♡
Pass	3 ♡	Pass	3 NT
Pass	4 ♣	Pass	4 ◇
Pass	4 ♠	Pass	5 ♣
Pass	6 ♡	All Pass	

One club was strong (17+ HCP) and artificial. 1NT conventionally showed four controls (A =2, K = 1). The next three
bids were natural, and then cue-bidding led to slam.

You, West, lead the ◇Q. Declarer wins the king and plays the
♠4 to dummy's king, East following with the nine. The ♣K is
cashed, and declarer continues with a heart to his king and the
♡J. What do you discard on this trick?

24. Dlr: South   ♠ A 6
         Vul: Both   ♡ K 10 8 7 4
                          ◇ K 10 9
                          ♣ 8 7 5

                                        ♠ Q 8 5 3
                                        ♡ Q 5 3
                          □   ◇ A 2
                                        ♣ J 10 9 2

WEST	NORTH	EAST	SOUTH
			1 NT
Pass	2 ◇[1]	Pass	2 ♡
Pass	3 NT[2]	Pass	4 ♡
All Pass			

[1] a 'transfer' bid that conventionally asks opener to bid 2♡
[2] offers a choice of games

West, your partner, leads the ♠J, won by declarer's king. At trick two, the ♡9 is led, partner and dummy play low, and you take your queen. How do you continue?

Solutions (C)

21. Lead a low diamond. Declarer would have been obliged to duck the first trick if he had Q-x.

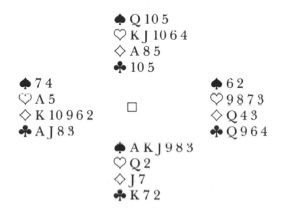

```
              ♠ Q 10 5
              ♡ K J 10 6 4
              ◇ A 8 5
              ♣ 10 5
♠ 7 4                              ♠ 6 2
♡ A 5                              ♡ 9 8 7 3
◇ K 10 9 6 2        □             ◇ Q 4 3
♣ A J 8 3                          ♣ Q 9 6 4
              ♠ A K J 9 8 3
              ♡ Q 2
              ◇ J 7
              ♣ K 7 2
```

Winning the ◇Q, partner knows he must play you for the ♣A for the fourth defensive trick. He will return a low club (promising an honour), and you will have no trouble cashing two club tricks.

22. From the club play, declarer is marked with the ace, so East must have the ◇A. Switch to a low diamond, since you may need to cash out.

```
              ♠ Q 7 5 2
              ♡ A 10 7 5
              ◇ Q 10 6
              ♣ 7 5
♠ A 10 6                          ♠ K J 9 8 3
♡ 9 3                             ♡ J 2
◇ K 7 5 4 2        □             ◇ A J 9
♣ Q J 4                           ♣ K 6 2
              ♠ 4
              ♡ K Q 8 6 4
              ◇ 8 3
              ♣ A 10 9 8 3
```

If you carelessly continue with a third spade, declarer will ruff, cash the ♣A, establish clubs with a ruff, draw trumps, and discard two diamonds from dummy, making the contract.

23.   Why did declarer play spades before drawing trumps? If he had a guess in the suit (with, say, Q-10-x), he would have put it off as long as possible. (In any case, if he had a guess he has guessed correctly.) It is more likely that declarer led an early spade to prepare for an end-play before you realized there was danger. The full deal:

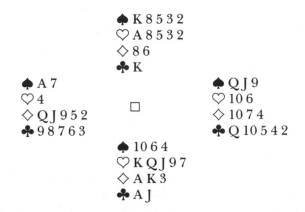

In a 1970 tournament, Victor Mitchell discarded the ♠A on the second trump, defeating the contract.

Declarer could have made the slam by stripping the minors and leading a spade after playing just one trump. West could have defeated it (rather less spectacularly) by winning the first spade.

24.   Declarer has at least an eight-card heart fit. If he had A-x-x, he would cash the ace and king, or at least cash the ace first. With A-J-x he certainly would cash the ace before finessing. So it seems partner must have the ♡A. In that case, there is no point in leading a club, since partner can have no points in the suit. Switch to ace and another diamond, trying for a ruff.

```
                    ♠ A 6
                    ♡ K 10 8 7 4
                    ◇ K 10 9
                    ♣ 8 7 5
♠ J 10 9 7                              ♠ Q 8 5 3
♡ A 2                  □                ♡ Q 5 3
◇ 8 7 6 5                               ◇ A 2
♣ 6 4 3                                ♣ J 10 9 2
                    ♠ K 4 2
                    ♡ J 9 6
                    ◇ Q J 4 3
                    ♣ A K Q
```

Quiz 20

Counting and More Counting

It's much easier to defend well when you know what declarer has. On many hands, in fact, producing the best defence will be impossible unless you keep close track of declarer's high cards, distribution, and playing tricks.

Clues to declarer's hands are always available. He must, for example, give you a peek at his holding in the bidding. To take the simplest example, a 1NT opening marks declarer with narrowly defined strength and pattern, so the defenders have a big head start on reconstructing his exact holding.

As the play proceeds, other bits of information surface: players will show out as suits are led, partner will signal his distribution, inferences will abound. Sometimes you'll know the whole story before the play is halfway over.

The most difficult hands are those on which you must make a crucial decision very early, before all the evidence is in. It is on such hands that you may have to try for an inferential or hypothetical count (see Quiz 21), make assumptions about the way the cards lie (see Quiz 8), or just venture your best guess.

Three different areas of counting require the defenders' attention. On the hand below, counting declarer's *high-card points* is the key to success.

Dlr: South   ♠ A Q J 9 4
Vul: Both   ♡ 8 6 3
               ◇ Q 7
               ♣ Q 10 3

♠ 10 7 2   ♠ 8 6 5
♡ K 10 5 2   □   ♡ A J 7
◇ J 10 9 8   ◇ 6 3 2
♣ A 4   ♣ J 9 7 5

               ♠ K 3
               ♡ Q 9 4
               ◇ A K 5 4
               ♣ K 8 6 2

WEST	NORTH	EAST	SOUTH
			1 ◇
Pass	1 ♠	Pass	1 NT
Pass	3 NT	All Pass	

West leads the ◇J. Dummy's queen wins, and declarer plays a club to the king and ace. West knows that declarer has at most 15 HCP, and he already has shown 10 – the ◇AK and ♣K. Therefore, declarer's hearts cannot be as good as ace-queen, and a heart play is at the very least safe. (Really, West would expect declarer to hold the ♠K – unless declarer's spades were ready to run, he would have won the first trick in hand to take a spade finesse, saving the ◇Q as a dummy entry. So declarer isn't likely to have even as much as the ♡A.)

Getting a count on declarer's *distribution* may require a knowledge of normal bidding methods.

Dlr: South
Vul: N-S

```
            ♠ Q 10
            ♡ A J 2
            ◇ K J 6 5 2
            ♣ 7 6 3
♠ K 3                      ♠ 8 7 2
♡ 7 6 4          □         ♡ Q 10 5
◇ A 7 3                    ◇ Q 9 8 4
♣ K 10 8 4 2               ♣ Q 9 5
            ♠ A J 9 6 5 4
            ♡ K 9 8 3
            ◇ 10
            ♣ A J
```

WEST	NORTH	EAST	SOUTH
			1 ♠
Pass	2 ◇	Pass	2 ♠
Pass	2 NT	Pass	3 ♡
Pass	4 ♠	All Pass	

North's last bid is rather optimistic, but that's not West's problem. West leads a club to the queen and ace. At trick two, declarer plays the ◇10.

Normally, South's sequence suggests six spades, four hearts, and a minimum opening bid. Declarer is marked with the ♣J from East's play of the queen, so the ◇10 must be a singleton.

West therefore plays the ace and cashes the ♣K. A heart switch always beats the contract now (ruining declarer's entries for a red-suit squeeze against East), but even if West never breaks the heart suit, declarer almost surely will go down.

Counting declarer's *tricks* may be most important of all. The big edge: If you know how many winners declarer has, you can tell whether to conduct an active or a passive defence. (See Quiz 9.)

```
Dlr:  North              ♠ 9 3
Vul:  N-S                ♡ A K 6 3 2
                         ◇ A J 6
                         ♣ 7 6 2
       ♠ A 5 2                          ♠ 8 7
       ♡ 9 8                            ♡ J 10 7 4
       ◇ 10 9 8 3         □             ◇ Q 5 4 2
       ♣ K J 9 3                        ♣ A 8 5
                         ♠ K Q J 10 6 4
                         ♡ Q 5
                         ◇ K 7
                         ♣ Q 10 4
```

WEST	NORTH	EAST	SOUTH
	1 ♡	Pass	1 ♠
Pass	1 NT	Pass	4 ♠
All Pass			

West leads the ◇10 against South's game. East covers dummy's jack with the queen, and declarer takes his king. He leads the ♠K to West's ace.

West knows that declarer has at least six spades on the bidding, and declarer's play suggests that his suit is solid except for the ace. Declarer has two top tricks in each red suit, so ten tricks are there unless East has the ♣A. On this occasion, a club switch is needed to beat the contract.

Problems

1. Dlr: West   ♠ K J 6 3
     Vul: N-S   ♡ A 4
                 ◇ Q J 9 6 4
                 ♣ J 4

♠ A 8 4
♡ K Q 9 7 3
◇ K 10 7   □
♣ A 9

WEST	NORTH	EAST	SOUTH
1 ♡	Dbl	4 ♡	4 ♠
All Pass			

Back to rubber bridge, Chicago scoring, or IMPs – try to set the contract. You, West, lead the ♡K. Declarer wins the ace and leads a trump to his queen and your ace. You try to cash the ♡Q, but declarer ruffs and draws two more trumps, partner discarding hearts. Next, declarer cashes the ◇A, partner playing the two, and continues with the ◇3. How do you defend?

2. Dlr: South   ♠ J 10 6 4
     Vul: Both   ♡ A Q 5
                 ◇ A 10 9 6
                 ♣ J 3

                            ♠ A 5
                            ♡ 7 6 4 2
              □   ◇ K Q 5 4
                            ♣ Q 10 5

WEST	NORTH	EAST	SOUTH
			1 ♠
Pass	3 ♠	Pass	4 ♠
All Pass			

West, your partner, leads the ♡10 to dummy's ace. When the ♠J is led, you take your ace and exit with a trump, partner following suit low to both tricks. Declarer cashes the ♡Q and ♡K, partner following with the nine and eight. Now the ◇J is led and passed to your queen. How do you defend?

Solutions

1.

	♠ K J 6 3	
	♡ A 4	
	◇ Q J 9 6 4	
	♣ J 4	

♠ A 8 4		♠ 9
♡ K Q 9 7 3	☐	♡ J 10 8 6 5
◇ K 10 7		◇ 8 5 2
♣ A 9		♣ Q 10 7 5

	♠ Q 10 7 5 2	
	♡ 2	
	◇ A 3	
	♣ K 8 6 3 2	

A count of declarer's tricks will keep you from hitting the panic button. He has four spades, one heart and four diamonds. So he must play clubs himself to make the contract, and there is no need for you to lay down the ♣A.

Look at it another way: Declarer had five spades and one heart, and therefore seven minor-suit cards. Even after he leads diamonds five times in all and throws some of his clubs away, he still will have two of them left. If East has the ♣K or the queen and ten, declarer will be forced to go down.

2.

	♠ J 10 6 4	
	♡ A Q 5	
	◇ A 10 9 6	
	♣ J 3	

♠ 7 2		♠ A 5
♡ 10 9 8	☐	♡ 7 6 4 2
◇ 8 7 2		◇ K Q 5 4
♣ A 9 8 6 4		♣ Q 10 5

	♠ K Q 9 8 3	
	♡ K J 3	
	◇ J 3	
	♣ K 7 2	

Return a diamond. Declarer has five spades and three hearts – therefore, five cards in clubs and diamonds combined. If he started with two diamonds and three clubs, a diamond return won't help him – it will only allow him to discard a club he could have ruffed in dummy. He still will go down if West has the ♣A.

Even if declarer has two clubs and three diamonds and avoids a second diamond loser, he can't make the contract unless he has the ♣A. And if declarer started with

♠ K Q 9 8 x
♡ K J x
◇ J x x
♣ A x,

he has woefully misplayed the hand. After stripping out the majors, he could have exited with ace and another club, snaring the defenders in an end-play.

Problems

3. Dlr: South
    Vul: E-W
    Matchpoints

    ♠ A K J
    ♡ K 6 3
    ◇ 8 6 3
    ♣ Q 10 7 3

    ♠ 10 9 8 5 3
    ♡ 7
    ◇ A J 7 5 2
    ♣ K 8

    □

WEST	NORTH	EAST	SOUTH
			Pass
Pass	1 ♣	Pass	1 ♡
Pass	1 NT	Pass	3 ♡¹
All Pass			

¹ invitational, not forcing

You, West, lead the ♠10. Declarer wins the ace, and East plays the seven. Declarer plays the ♡K and a heart to the ace, shrugging when you show out. He cashes the ♣A and continues a club to your king, East following with the four and six. How do you defend?

4. Dlr: South   ♠ J 9 3
    Vul: N-S   ♡ A J 4 3
                         ◇ Q J 6 5
                         ♣ A 10

♠ 6 5
♡ K Q 10 8   □
◇ K 7 2
♣ 5 4 3 2

WEST	NORTH	EAST	SOUTH
			1 ♠
Pass	2 NT	Pass	3 ♣
Pass	3 ♠	Pass	4 ♠
All Pass			

You, West, lead the ♡K – three, two, six. What do you lead to trick two?

Solutions

3.   Declarer will have a six-card heart suit for his jump, so you can place him with the ♡A and jack for 5 HCP. He already has shown the ♣A – that's 9 HCP – so he cannot have the ◇K. Even if he has the ◇Q, he has a hand some players would open. Lead a low diamond.

                    ♠ A K J
                    ♡ K 6 3
                    ◇ 8 6 3
                    ♣ Q 10 7 3

♠ 10 9 8 5 3   ♠ Q 7 2
♡ 7   ♡ Q 10 9
◇ A J 7 5 2   □   ◇ K 9
♣ K 8   ♣ J 9 6 5 4

                    ♠ 6 4
                    ♡ A J 8 5 4 2
                    ◇ Q 10 4
                    ♣ A 2

4.   Declarer's bidding suggests at least nine black cards – probably his pattern is 5-2-2-4. He would have no reason to duck the opening lead with a singleton heart, and if he had three hearts, it would be too dangerous to duck. You should shift to a diamond. Even if declarer has the $\diamondsuit$A, this play will cost you nothing. (Declarer would have finessed in hearts and discarded his little diamond anyhow.) However, if partner has the $\diamondsuit$A, you must cash your two diamond tricks right away before declarer can take a discard.

```
                    ♠ J 9 3
                    ♡ A J 4 3
                    ◇ Q J 6 5
                    ♣ A 10
   ♠ 6 5                              ♠ Q 10 8
   ♡ K Q 10 8                         ♡ 9 5 9
   ◇ K 7 2             ⊔              ◇ A 9 8 4
   ♣ 5 4 3 2                          ♣ J 8 7
                    ♠ A K 7 4 2
                    ♡ 7 6
                    ◇ 10 3
                    ♣ K Q 9 6
```

Quiz 21

A Problem-Solver's Game: Drawing Inferences

There is more to good bridge than just memorizing a set of rules or even paying heed to principles and tendencies. Bridge appeals because it is a game of problem-solving and logic.

Quiz 8 dealt with making assumptions in defence. As we saw, many assumptions amount to no more than hopeful speculation. An *inference*, however, is an assumption supported by the logical analysis of evidence.

If your opponents play logically and observe accepted practices and conventions, they'll reveal something about what they have and what their plans are. Useful inferences abound in the bidding and play. I can remember deals when I let a beatable contract slip through, and at the time I saw nothing to indicate the winning defence. Later, after some reflection, I realized I had missed a subtle but telling inference.

There are several sources of inferences. To start at trick one, analysis of the bidding may guide you to a killing opening lead. Suppose you hold as West:

♠ K 10
♡ A J 8 5 2
♢ J 4
♣ K Q 10 3

WEST	NORTH	EAST	SOUTH
1 ♡	Pass	1 ♠	Pass
2 ♣	Pass	Pass	2 ♢
All Pass			

Partner bid spades, but the ♠K would be a poor lead when he must have a very weak hand. A better shot is to find him short in hearts – he failed to raise directly or even take a preference over your 2♣ rebid. Perhaps half the time, partner will hold a singleton heart, so ♡A and another is an attractive form of attack. The full deal might be:

```
                    ♠ 8 5 3
                    ♡ K Q 10 3
                    ♢ A 8 2
                    ♣ 9 6 4
   ♠ K 10                        ♠ Q 9 7 6 4
   ♡ A J 8 5 2        □          ♡ 4
   ♢ J 4                         ♢ 9 6 3
   ♣ K Q 10 3                    ♣ A 8 5 2
                    ♠ A J 2
                    ♡ 9 7 6
                    ♢ K Q 10 7 5
                    ♣ J 7
```

After ♡A, ♡2, East can put you back in twice with clubs for further ruffs neutralising dummy's hearts. Then declarer will have to manoeuvre an endplay to escape with just one down.

If you can assume partner is thinking clearly, some valid inferences may be available from *his* opening lead and subsequent defence.

```
Dlr: East           ♠ Q 10 5
Vul: None           ♡ K 9 6 3
                    ♢ Q 8 2
                    ♣ J 9 3
   ♠ A 6 2                        ♠ K J 9 7 3
   ♡ 8 4              □           ♡ J 2
   ♢ J 7 6 4 3                    ♢ A 10 5
   ♣ 10 8 5                       ♣ A 7 2
                    ♠ 8 4
                    ♡ A Q 10 7 5
                    ♢ K 9
                    ♣ K Q 6 4
```

WEST	NORTH	EAST	SOUTH
		1 ♠	2 ♡
2 ♠	3 ♡	All Pass	

This was at matchpoints. West led the ♢4, and East took the ace.

Reluctant to lead away from the ♠K despite partner's raise, East returned a low club. This allowed declarer to make a valuable overtrick by drawing trumps and depositing a spade on the ♢Q.

Players are reluctant to lay down aces, even in a suit partner has bid, for fear of setting up an intermediate card for declarer. (Here, West doubtless reasoned that there always would be time to cash E-W's spade tricks, since East had opened the bidding and had to have some entries.) East therefore should have played partner for the ♠A and led a spade at trick two. If West had held three or four small spades, would not his opening lead have been a spade?

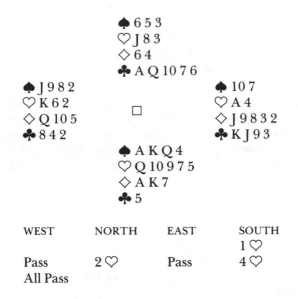

```
                  ♠ 6 5 3
                  ♡ J 8 3
                  ♢ 6 4
                  ♣ A Q 10 7 6
 ♠ J 9 8 2                          ♠ 10 7
 ♡ K 6 2                            ♡ A 4
 ♢ Q 10 5            □              ♢ J 9 8 3 2
 ♣ 8 4 2                            ♣ K J 9 3
                  ♠ A K Q 4
                  ♡ Q 10 9 7 5
                  ♢ A K 7
                  ♣ 5
```

WEST	NORTH	EAST	SOUTH
			1 ♡
Pass	2 ♡	Pass	4 ♡
All Pass			

For lack of anything better, West leads a low trump. East wins the ace and returns a trump. Now West should lead a third round. Should he not be afraid of dummy's club suit? No — unless East had the clubs all sewed up, he surely would have switched to a diamond or spade.

```
              ♠ K J 5 4
              ♡ K J 4 3
              ◇ 9 6 3
              ♣ Q 5
♠ 8 7 2                          ♠ 10 6 3
♡ Q 10 8            □            ♡ 9 7 5
◇ A 5 4                          ◇ K 10 8 7 2
♣ J 9 6 2                        ♣ A 7
              ♠ A Q 9
              ♡ A 6 2
              ◇ Q J
              ♣ K 10 8 4 3
```

WEST	NORTH	EAST	SOUTH
			1 NT
Pass	3 NT	All Pass	

West led the ♣2 – five, ace, three. East expected declarer to
have either the ♣J or king, since declarer might have put up
dummy's queen if lacking both of those honours. East decided to
shift to a diamond – but was it the right time for the
honour-trapping lead of the *ten*?

East knew that declarer had five clubs. The lead of the ten
might save a trick if declarer had three diamonds, but that
meant he would have only two cards in one of the majors. West
then would have had a four-card major suit, and he likely would
have preferred to lead that suit instead of a club. So East
rejected the tempting 'surrounding' play and led a pedestrian
◇7, playing declarer for 3-3-2-5 pattern. As you can see, the
fancy lead of the ten would have caused a disaster this time.

On the next hand, several inferences are available.

```
              ♠ Q J 10 5
              ♡ K J 5
              ◇ 10 8
              ♣ A K 5 2
♠ 3 2                           ♠ A K 7
♡ A 10 8 4 2        □           ♡ 9 6
◇ 7 5 3                         ◇ Q J 9 6 2
♣ J 10 9                        ♣ 8 4 3
              ♠ 9 8 6 4
              ♡ Q 7 3
              ◇ A K 4
              ♣ Q 7 6
```

WEST	NORTH	EAST	SOUTH
	1 ♣	Pass	1 ♠
Pass	2 ♣	Pass	2 NT
Pass	4 ♠	All Pass	

West leads the ♣J. Declarer wins in dummy and leads the ♠Q to East's king. Back comes the ♡9. If West wins and returns a heart, the defence is through except for the ♠A. However, if West thinks about it, the right play of ducking is clear.

The bidding strongly suggests that declarer has only four spades (and East's defence would make no sense unless he had a small trump with which to ruff). But if East's ♡9 is singleton, then declarer has four hearts and would have responded one heart to one club, bidding his major suits 'up the line'.

Finally, if East had a singleton heart, he should *cash the* ♠*A* before leading his heart, giving West no choice but to win and return the suit.

On that deal, West can get an *inferential* count of the distribution. Here's another example of the technique. Suppose that East hears this bidding:

WEST	NORTH	EAST	SOUTH
			1 NT
Pass	2 ♣	Pass	2 ♡
Pass	2 ♠	Pass	2 NT

West leads the ♢2. East's pattern is 4-3-2-4, while dummy discloses a 5-2-3-3 shape. Right away, East can deduce that declarer is 2-4-4-3.

Another illustration:

```
                    ♠ A 7 4
                    ♡ A J 6 3
                    ♢ K J 6 2
                    ♣ 7 2
    ♠ J 9 6 5                      ♠ K 3 2
    ♡ Q 10 4                       ♡ 9 7 5 2
    ♢ 7 5          □               ♢ A 10
    ♣ K 10 6 3                     ♣ J 9 5 4
                    ♠ Q 10 8
                    ♡ K 8
                    ♢ Q 9 8 4 3
                    ♣ A Q 8
```

WEST	NORTH	EAST	SOUTH
			1 ◇
Pass	1 ♡	Pass	1 NT
Pass	3 ◇	Pass	3 NT
All Pass			

West leads a spade, ducked to the king. Before leading to the next trick, East tries to deduce declarer's pattern. Declarer did not rebid 1♠, nor did he raise hearts directly or show a preference when invited to. Therefore, he should have at most two hearts and three spades. (West's lead indicates that declarer has exactly three spades.) If declarer had been 4-4 in the minors, he probably would have opened 1♣ – there is little point to opening in the higher ranking of two four-card minor suits when you plan to rebid 1NT. So East is inclined to place declarer with a five-card diamond suit, and he can assume that declarer has the ♣Q for his 3 NT bid.

Desperate measures are needed. The spade suit won't provide enough tricks to beat the contract, and a passive defence isn't a favourite, either – declarer's long suit should let him set up nine tricks eventually. So East shifts aggressively to the ♣J – and this time he strikes gold.

Defenders must take careful note of unusual plays by declarer. If a capable declarer does something a bit out of the ordinary, you can bet he has something up his sleeve.

Dlr: South   ♠ A Q 6
Vul: E-W   ♡ A Q J 9 5
               ◇ 10 4
               ♣ J 10 2

♠ 8 7 2   ♠ K J 10 5
♡ 7 6 3   ♡ 10 8 4
◇ Q 9 8 3   □   ◇ K J 2
♣ K 7 4   ♣ 8 6 5

               ♠ 9 4 3
               ♡ K 2
               ◇ A 7 6 5
               ♣ A Q 9 3

WEST	NORTH	EAST	SOUTH
			1 ♣
Pass	1 ♡	Pass	1 NT
Pass	3 NT	All Pass	

Unwilling to break the diamond suit, West leads the ♠8. Declarer considers going up with the ace, but he fears that East has five spades. Finally, he concocts an alternative scheme – he plays dummy's queen. If East wins and returns a spade, declarer will win and take a club finesse – he knows that if West produces the ♣K and has a spade left to lead, the defenders will take only four tricks in all.

East should wonder why declarer didn't play *low* from dummy at trick one, keeping dummy's spade tenace intact and gaining some time. The most likely explanation – declarer is nervous about some other suit and wants to make it easy for the defenders to continue spades! So East finds the good switch to a diamond honour, and down declarer goes.

Problems

1. Dlr: South
    Vul: N-S

    ♠ A 10 5 2
    ♡ 7 3
    ◇ 8 5
    ♣ J 10 6 5 2

    ♠ K 8 3
    ♡ Q 9 5 2
    ◇ A Q 10 6 4
    ♣ 3

    □

WEST	NORTH	EAST	SOUTH
			1 ♠
Dbl (!)	2 ♠	3 ♣	4 ♠
All Pass			

You, West, lead the ♣3. East obliges with the ace, and declarer drops the queen. You ruff the ♣9 return, declarer playing the king. How do you continue?

2. Dlr: South
    Vul: E-W

    ♠ Q 10 7 3
    ♡ Q 6 4
    ◇ A J 6 3
    ♣ 7 6

    ♠ 6 2
    ♡ K 9 8 5 2
    ◇ Q 9 2
    ♣ A 9 2

    □

WEST	NORTH	EAST	SOUTH
			1 ♣
Pass	1 ♠	Pass	2 NT
Pass	3 NT	All Pass	

You, West, lead the ♡5 – six, ten, jack. Declarer plays off the ♠AK and continues with a spade to the queen; East follows high-low as you discard a club. Now the ◇A is cashed and a diamond is led to the seven, ten, and your queen. Do you get out passively with a diamond, risk a heart continuation, or break new ground in the club suit?

Solutions

1.

```
                    ♠ A 10 5 2
                    ♡ 7 3
                    ◇ 8 5
                    ♣ J 10 6 5 2
    ♠ K 8 3                       ♠ 7
    ♡ Q 9 5 2            ☐        ♡ K 10 6
    ◇ A Q 10 6 4                  ◇ 9 7 3 2
    ♣ 3                           ♣ A 9 8 7 4
                    ♠ Q J 9 6 4
                    ♡ A J 8 4
                    ◇ K J
                    ♣ K Q
```

Having made a takeout double of 1♠, you can be counted on for four cards in the other major. The key clue is that East did not compete in hearts, as he surely would have done with four of them. So declarer is likely to have four hearts in addition to his (probably five) spades.

You must cash the ◇A. If you don't, declarer will throw his diamonds on dummy's clubs. Hearts, however, can wait – if declarer has a heart loser, he will be unable to avoid it.

2. Continue with a low heart. Declarer is marked with three spades. His method of attacking diamonds suggests he has four cards there – if he had only three diamonds, he has left a winner stranded in dummy! Declarer must have at least four clubs – he would have opened 1◇ otherwise. Therefore, he should have just two hearts, and a heart continuation is safe.

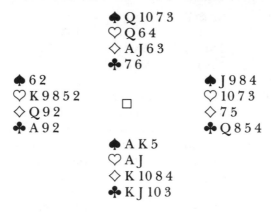

♠ Q 10 7 3
♡ Q 6 4
◇ A J 6 3
♣ 7 6

♠ 6 2   ♠ J 9 8 4
♡ K 9 8 5 2   ♡ 10 7 3
◇ Q 9 2   ◇ 7 5
♣ A 9 2   ♣ Q 8 5 4

♠ A K 5
♡ A J
◇ K 10 8 4
♣ K J 10 3

If you gamble with a diamond, declarer might win in dummy and play a club to his jack, setting up the ninth trick.

Problems

3. Dlr: South   ♠ K 9 3
    Vul: Both   ♡ 5 4 3 2
               ◇ J
               ♣ A Q 10 8 3

♠ 7 2
♡ J 10 7 6
◇ A 10 8 3
♣ 9 7 2

WEST	NORTH	EAST	SOUTH
			1 ♠
Pass	2 ♣	Pass	2 ◇
Pass	2 ♠	Pass	3 ♠
All Pass			

You, West, lead the ♡6 – two, queen, ace. At trick two, declarer leads a low diamond. Plan your defence.

4. Dlr: South   ♠ 7 5
        Vul: N-S   ♡ A J 5 4
                         ◇ Q J 10 4
                         ♣ Q 7 5

   ♠ K 10 6 2
   ♡ 7 6   □
   ◇ A 8 7
   ♣ K J 9 4

WEST	NORTH	EAST	SOUTH
			1 ♡
Dbl	Redbl	Pass	Pass
1 ♠	2 ♡	Pass	4 ♡
All Pass			

You, West, choose a trump lead. Declarer draws two rounds, partner following, and plays the ◇K. You win the second diamond, East playing high-low. How do you continue?

Solutions

3. For starters, grab the ◇A – declarer could easily have the king and queen. Then switch to a trump. Declarer's diamond play indicates that he is interested in ruffing losers in dummy. If instead he wanted to make use of dummy's clubs, he would be trying to draw trumps himself.

                    ♠ K 9 3
                    ♡ 5 4 3 2
                    ◇ J
                    ♣ A Q 10 8 3
   ♠ 7 2   ♠ A Q 4
   ♡ J 10 7 6   □   ♡ Q 8
   ◇ A 10 8 3   ◇ 9 7 6 4
   ♣ 9 7 2   ♣ K J 6 4
                    ♠ J 10 8 6 5
                    ♡ A K 9
                    ◇ K Q 5 2
                    ♣ 5

On your trump switch, partner will clear three rounds, leaving declarer a trick short of his contract.

It is true that a very subtle declarer might lead a diamond, trying to induce you to lead trumps and resolve a guess in the trump suit for him. Luckily, there aren't many declarers around who are that tricky.

4. When North redoubled, East's first duty was to bail your side out to a playable spot if he could. When he failed to bid 1♠, he patently denied four cards in spades, so you can place declarer with four. East petered in diamonds, so declarer's pattern probably is 4-5-2-2.

You must realize that a club switch cannot lose even if declarer has the ace. Declarer always could throw his clubs on dummy's diamonds and lose at most two spade tricks, making the contract. However, two *spade* discards on the diamonds won't help declarer – he'd just be throwing away cards that he just as easily could ruff in dummy. The full deal:

```
                    ♠ 7 5
                    ♡ A J 5 4
                    ◇ Q J 10 4
                    ♣ Q 7 5
    ♠ K 10 6 2                    ♠ 9 8 3
    ♡ 7 6                         ♡ 10 2
    ◇ A 8 7          □            ◇ 9 6 3 2
    ♣ K J 9 4                     ♣ A 8 3 2
                    ♠ A Q J 4
                    ♡ K Q 9 8 3
                    ◇ K 5
                    ♣ 10 6
```

With declarer holding the ♣10, the ♣J lead (or the ♣K followed by the ♣J) is needed to beat the contract.

Quiz 22

Picking Up Partner

It's common knowledge that most partners need all the help they can get. Bridge is a partnership game, and like it or not, our results depend on what that person across the table does. Regardless of what sadistic impulses we may harbour, winning bridge means helping partner avoid mistakes.

Players often forget that a good partner will take note of every little thing that happens at the table – for instance, he will watch the spot cards like a hawk, looking for subtle inferences. In the simple situation below, East would have to consider his partner's problems to avoid a potentially costly play.

```
              A 7 6
  9 3          □          J 8 5 4 2
              K Q 10
```

West leads the nine of this suit, and dummy ducks. If East plays the jack and declarer wins the king, the position will be unclear to West – he may cherish the belief that he has found partner with the queen-jack and continue the suit in vain. If East wants to make sure that West loses interest in this suit, he should play the two.

```
Dlr: North        ♠ Q 7
Vul: None         ♡ K 6 3
                  ◇ 9 7 5
                  ♣ A K J 10 4
  ♠ K 3                            ♠ 8 5 2
  ♡ 9 8 5 4 2         □            ♡ A Q
  ◇ 8 3                            ◇ K Q J 6 4 2
  ♣ 9 8 6 3                        ♣ 7 5
                  ♠ A J 10 9 6 4
                  ♡ J 10 7
                  ◇ A 10
                  ♣ Q 2
```

WEST	NORTH	EAST	SOUTH
	1 ♣	1 ♢	1 ♠
Pass	2 ♣	Pass	3 ♠
Pass	4 ♠	All Pass	

West leads the ♢8. East can see that there is little hope for the defence unless West has a trump trick and he can be encouraged to switch to hearts. So East unconventionally plays the ♢K at trick one. When West wins the ♠K, he will place declarer with the ♢Q, and a heart switch will be much more attractive.

Perhaps West should find the heart switch in any case, but East is trying to preserve his partner's supply of mental energy for other hands yet to come.

This deal, from one of Alfred Sheinwold's fine books, illustrates the same idea.

```
                    ♠ 10 5
                    ♡ 7 4 3
                    ♢ K J 8 3
                    ♣ K Q J 3
    ♠ A 9 8 6 4                    ♠ K Q
    ♡ 8 5 2                        ♡ J 10 9 6
    ♢ A 6 4          □             ♢ 7 5 2
    ♣ 7 5                          ♣ 9 8 6 2
                    ♠ J 7 3 2
                    ♡ A K Q
                    ♢ Q 10 9
                    ♣ A 10 4
```

West leads the ♠6 against 3 NT, and East holds the first two tricks with the queen and king. Now the defence can take no more than West's two aces, and the contract is made.

As the cards lie, West could have beaten the contract by overtaking the ♠K and leading the nine. Declarer cannot get home without a diamond trick. When a diamond is led, West takes his ace and cashes two more spades. However, as West protested, this defence would be spectacularly unsuccessful if declarer's hand were

```
                    ♠ J 3 2
                    ♡ A K Q 6
                    ♢ Q 10 9
                    ♣ A 10 4
```

Sheinwold points out that East was mainly at fault for putting partner to a guess. He should have played his spade honours out of order – the king first, then the queen. The message that he had only two cards in the suit would have been clear.

Declarer made another impossible game on the next deal. Which defender do you think was more to blame?

```
Dlr: South        ♠ Q 3
Vul: N-S          ♡ 10 7 4
                  ◇ A 7
                  ♣ A J 9 5 4 2
   ♠ A 9 7 6                    ♠ 10 8 5 4
   ♡ A J 8                      ♡ K 9 6 2
   ◇ J 9 8 2         □          ◇ 10 6
   ♣ Q 8                        ♣ 7 6 3
                  ♠ K J 2
                  ♡ Q 5 3
                  ◇ K Q 5 4 3
                  ♣ K 10
```

WEST	NORTH	EAST	SOUTH
			1 ◇
Pass	2 ♣	Pass	2 NT
Pass	3 NT	All Pass	

West led the ♠6. Dummy's queen held, East playing the five. Declarer tried a club to the ten and queen. Now West found the killing shift to the ♡8, but East, on winning the king, switched back to spades. The defence could take no more than four tricks.

We hold East almost blameless. West just as easily could have held

```
                  ♠ A J x x
                  ♡ A 8 x
                  ◇ J 9 x x
                  ♣ Q x
```

(although with that hand he might have laid down the ♡A first). As East argued in the post-mortem, if West wanted a spade return, it *would* be correct for him to lead a high heart to discourage a heart continuation – and the eight looked pretty high.

Perhaps West should have removed partner's losing option by *cashing the* ♠*A* before shifting to hearts.

Problems

1.   Dlr: South   ♠ A 6
        Vul: Both   ♡ 7 6
                          ◇ K J 7 2
                          ♣ A Q 10 6 5

                                                ♠ K 3
                                                ♡ A K 8 5 2
                    □   ◇ Q 10 4 3
                                                ♣ 9 7

WEST	NORTH	EAST	SOUTH
			3 ♠
Pass	4 ♠	All Pass	

West, your partner, leads the ♡Q. How do you defend?

2.   Dlr: North   ♠ 9 6
        Vul: Both   ♡ A K Q 7 5
                          ◇ Q 3
                          ♣ K Q 8 3

        ♠ 5 3 2
        ♡ 9 8 4 2
        ◇ K 8 6 5 2   □
        ♣ 2

WEST	NORTH	EAST	SOUTH
	1 ♡	Pass	1 ♠
Pass	2 ♣	Pass	3 ♠
Pass	4 ♠	All Pass	

You, West, lead your singleton club. Partner obligingly captures dummy's king with the ace and returns the ♣4, which you ruff. Declarer has followed with the seven and ten. How do you continue?

Solutions

1. Overtake with the ♡K, cash the ♡A, and lead a diamond. If you leave West on lead, he may shift to clubs or underlead the ◇A. Remember, he cannot know that you are looking at a surprise trick in trumps.

```
                   ♠ A 6
                   ♡ 7 6
                   ◇ K J 7 2
                   ♣ A Q 10 6 5
    ♠ 9 7                           ♠ K 3
    ♡ Q J 9                         ♡ A K 8 5 2
    ◇ A 0 8 5        □              ◇ Q 10 4 3
    ♣ J 8 3 2                       ♣ 9 7
                   ♠ Q J 10 8 5 4 2
                   ♡ 10 4 3
                   ◇ 6
                   ♣ K 4
```

2.
```
                   ♠ 9 6
                   ♡ A K Q 7 5
                   ◇ Q 3
                   ♣ K Q 8 3
    ♠ 5 3 2                         ♠ J 7
    ♡ 9 8 4 2                       ♡ 10 3
    ◇ K 8 6 5 2      □              ◇ A 10 7
    ♣ 2                             ♣ A J 9 6 5 4
                   ♠ A K Q 10 8 4
                   ♡ J 6
                   ◇ J 9 4
                   ♣ 10 7
```

Lead the ◇K. Partner's ♣4 is a suit-preference signal requesting a diamond return – presumably, he has the ◇A. However, if you return a low diamond, you give him a problem. He might decide to play you for the ♠Q instead of the ◇K. (Indeed, with that defence, he *should*.) If he returns a third round of clubs, trying for a trump promotion, declarer will ruff high, draw trumps, and claim.

Problems

3. Dlr: East   ♠ 9 3
    Vul: N-S   ♡ K Q 8 5 4 3
                       ◇ A 5 3
                       ♣ Q 5
                                      ♠ K J 10 8 6 4
                                      ♡ A 10
                           □   ◇ 4
                                      ♣ A 7 4 2

WEST	NORTH	EAST	SOUTH
		1 ♠	2 ◇
4 ♠	5 ◇	Dbl	All Pass

West, your partner, leads the ♡2. Plan your defence.

4. Dlr: North   ♠ J 9 5 3
    Vul: Both   ♡ 8 7
                       ◇ A K Q
                       ♣ K J 10 4
    ♠ 7
    ♡ J 10 9 6 3
    ◇ J 8 2   □
    ♣ A 8 6 2

WEST	NORTH	EAST	SOUTH
	1 ♣	Pass	1 ♠
Pass	2 ♠	Pass	3 ♠
Pass	4 ♠	All Pass	

You, West, lead the ♡J – seven, two, king. Declarer plays a trump to the jack. East wins the king and returns the ♣9. How do you defend?

Solutions

3.

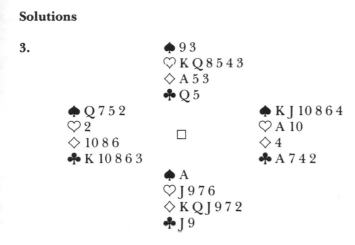

No disasters! Cash the ♣A at trick two, then give partner his heart ruff. If you return the ♡10 immediately, partner is likely to return a spade, your bid suit, after ruffing. (Note that a suit-preference mix-up is likely because fate dealt you just one heart with the ace, and it happens to be a high one. Declarer could add to the confusion by following with the nine and jack on the two heart leads.)

4. Declarer would take a finesse if he were missing only the ♠K, so East must hold the ace also. If you trust your partner, you will duck the club, playing him for a doubleton. If partner had a singleton club, he would have cashed his ♠A before leading it, removing your option of ducking.

```
                    ♠ J 9 5 3
                    ♡ 8 7
                    ◇ A K Q
                    ♣ K J 10 4
    ♠ 7                              ♠ A K 2
    ♡ J 10 9 6 3         □          ♡ Q 5 4 2
    ◇ J 8 2                         ◇ 10 9 6 5
    ♣ A 8 6 2                       ♣ 9 5
                    ♠ Q 10 8 6 4
                    ♡ A K
                    ◇ 7 4 3
                    ♣ Q 7 3
```

Quiz 23

A Touch of the High Life: Deception

Although this is one area of play where new wrinkles are uncovered every so often, volumes and volumes already have been written on how to fool declarer. There are innumerable positions where a false-card is desirable, and still others where one is mandatory.

The J-9 combination is associated with many false-cards:

$$\begin{array}{ccc} & 10\,8\,2 & \\ \text{K}\,5\,4\,3 & \square & \text{J}\,9 \\ & \text{A}\,\text{Q}\,7\,6 & \end{array}$$

Declarer leads the two from dummy. If East plays the nine, declarer's queen loses to the king. But the jack drops under the ace next, giving declarer three tricks. Note the effect if East plays his jack on the *first* round. Declarer's queen will lose to the king again, but on regaining the lead declarer will finesse dummy's eight, playing West for K-9-5-4-3.

$$\begin{array}{ccc} & \text{K}\,\text{Q}\,10\,8\,4\,2 & \\ \text{A}\,7\,3 & \square & \text{J}\,9 \\ & 6\,5 & \end{array}$$

Needing to set up this suit, declarer leads low to the king. Say East follows with the nine. Declarer sees that if West has A-J-7-3, two tricks must be lost in any case, so he comes back to hand and leads low to the queen. But if East drops his jack on the first lead, declarer surely will play to dummy's eight next.

$$\begin{array}{ccc} & 10\,7\,6\,3 & \\ \text{K} & \square & \text{A}\,\text{J}\,9 \\ & \text{Q}\,8\,5\,4\,2 & \end{array}$$

This suit is trumps, and declarer leads low from dummy. If East follows with the nine, declarer may duck, playing West for a singleton honour. But suppose East deviously plays the jack! Declarer will surely cover with the queen, and the defence will take three tricks.

A 10 8 4

J 9 5 2   □   3

K Q 7 6

Declarer, who is known to have four cards in this suit, starts by leading low to his king. If West follows with the two, declarer has no choice but to continue with the queen from hand, and the third-round finesse against West will become marked. However, West can offer declarer a losing option by dropping his *nine* on the first round. If the nine is in fact a singleton, declarer must play to the ace next to set up a finessing position against East.

The J-9 situations are part of one big family of deceptive plays. Q-9 holdings belong to another branch.

10 8 2

A 5 4   □   Q 9

K J 7 6 3

Declarer leads low from dummy, and East must play the queen.

On board 77 of the 1976 Bermuda Bowl final, the contract at one table was 3♠ and the trump suit was:

10 6 5 3

A   □   Q J 9

K 8 7 4 2

When dummy led a trump at one point, East, Benito Garozzo, deceptively played the *queen*. This beautiful move failed to gain a trick only because Hugh Ross, the U.S. declarer, had a good idea where the missing high cards were from the bidding. He ducked in hand, refuting Garozzo's gambit.

Even the 10-8 tandem may come in for a share of deception.

K J 7 6

2   □   A 10 8 3

Q 9 5 4

Declarer leads low to dummy's jack. If East wins the ace, declarer will cash the king next, catering for A-10-8-3 in East. So East should let the jack hold, offering his *eight*. Declarer will probably lead back to his queen, expecting West to have A-10-3-2.

	K J 7 6	
A 10 8	□	Q 5 4
	9 3 2	

If declarer leads low toward dummy, West might produce a third trick from thin air by following with the *ten*. Assuming that the jack loses to the queen and the defenders place the lead in dummy, declarer may proceed to run the seven, playing East for Q-8-5-4 or A-Q-8-5-4.

Following with a higher card than you need to is the idea behind other deceptive plays. On the next deal, East pulled off a beautiful swindle.

Dlr: South
Vul: None

```
                    ♠ 10 5 4
                    ♡ 10 7 5 3
                    ◇ Q J 10 6
                    ♣ A Q
  ♠ A J 6 2                         ♠ K 9 7 3
  ♡ 9 6 2                           ♡ K J 8
  ◇ 8 7            □                ◇ K 5 2
  ♣ 9 8 6 4                         ♣ 10 7 2
                    ♠ Q 8
                    ♡ A Q 4
                    ◇ A 9 4 3
                    ♣ K J 5 3
```

WEST	NORTH	EAST	SOUTH
			1 NT
Pass	2 ♣	Pass	2 ◇
Pass	3 NT	All Pass	

This was the auction at both tables in a team-of-four match. At one table West led the normal spade, and the defenders took the first four tricks. Declarer saw that the contract depended on the location of the ◇K, so he discarded hearts from his hand and dummy. Winning the heart shift, he cashed the ♣A and ♣Q and took the diamond finesse for his contract.

At the other table West preferred to lead a passive ♡9. Dummy played low and East followed with the *jack*. Declarer eyed this card hopefully, won the ♡Q, and followed with the ace. Sure enough, East dropped the *king*.

Declarer now thought he was home – he could finesse the ♡7 for a fourth heart trick, and there were five top tricks available in the minors. But when East produced the ♡8, the defence took four spades for down one.

Winning a trick with a higher card than necessary sometimes can produce strange results.

```
              Q 10 9
   6 5 4        □           K J 3
              A 8 7 2
```

Declarer attacks this suit by leading low to the nine. If East wins the jack, declarer will lead the queen from dummy later, picking up the suit. Winning the king, however, would induce declarer to finesse the ten next in case West has J-x-x-x.

On other occasions a defender may do best not to win a trick at all.

Dlr: North ♠ J 5
Vul: Both   ♡ A J 6
      ♢ A Q J 3 2
      ♣ A J 5

♠ Q 10 8 2   ♠ K 7 6 3
♡ Q 9 4 3   ♡ 10 7 5
♢ 8 7   □   ♢ K 10 4
♣ Q 10 9   ♣ K 7 2

      ♠ A 9 4
      ♡ K 8 2
      ♢ 9 6 5
      ♣ 8 6 4 3

WEST	NORTH	EAST	SOUTH
	1 ♢	Pass	1 NT
Pass	3 NT	All Pass	

West leads the ♠2 to the jack, king, and ace. Declarer

immediately finesses the $\diamondsuit$Q, and East should *duck*. (However, the effect is lost unless he makes up his mind in advance to play low *without pause*.) Now declarer doesn't know whether to repeat the diamond finesse for the ninth trick or switch to hearts and try the finesse in that suit – and with only one entry left to his hand, he can't do both.

Opportunities for deception on the opening lead are common. For example, suppose you are on lead against 3 NT with K-Q-J-10-4 of spades and no other high cards. You might steal a trick by leading the *queen*. A possible deal, at matchpoint duplicate:

Dlr: East
Vul: N-S
Matchpoints

		$\spadesuit$ 7 6 3	
		$\heartsuit$ K 4	
		$\diamondsuit$ 5 3	
		$\clubsuit$ A J 9 6 5 3	
$\spadesuit$ K Q J 10 4			$\spadesuit$ 8 5
$\heartsuit$ 8 7 2		□	$\heartsuit$ 10 9 6 5 3
$\diamondsuit$ 9 8 6			$\diamondsuit$ A K 10 7
$\clubsuit$ 8 7			$\clubsuit$ K 4
		$\spadesuit$ A 9 2	
		$\heartsuit$ A Q J	
		$\diamondsuit$ Q J 4 2	
		$\clubsuit$ Q 10 2	

WEST	NORTH	EAST	SOUTH
		Pass	1 NT
Pass	3 NT	All Pass	

If the opening lead is the $\spadesuit$K, declarer will realize that holding up the ace once is free – even if the club finesse works, only ten tricks are available. But suppose West leads the spade *queen*. Now declarer may take a different view. If the queen is a true card, holding up twice cannot gain – if East, a passed hand, has both black kings, West must have a diamond honour for an entry. And when East plays low on the first spade, declarer may not even hold up once, sensing that East has forgotten to unblock with K-x.

Problems

Here is a departure from the usual format. In each problem, a full deal, a bidding sequence, and (except in Problem 1) an opening lead are shown. You must visualize the likely course of the play and spot a defender's chance for deception.

The problems would be too easy if we led you along and asked for your play at the critical point – and we're sure you wouldn't appreciate it if we made things too simple.

1. Dlr: South
   Vul: N-S

```
              ♠ K 7 3
              ♡ K J 3
              ◇ Q 6 4
              ♣ J 10 9 5
♠ J 9 6 2                      ♠ 8 4
♡ A 9 7 2          □          ♡ 10 8 6 5
◇ A 10 8                       ◇ J 9 7 2
♣ A 4                          ♣ 8 7 6
              ♠ A Q 10 5
              ♡ Q 4
              ◇ K 5 3
              ♣ K Q 3 2
```

WEST	NORTH	EAST	SOUTH
			1 NT
Pass	3 NT	All Pass	

The contract went down one. What was West's opening lead?

2. Dlr: West
   Vul: Both

```
              ♠ 10 7 5 2
              ♡ K 7 5 2
              ◇ K Q
              ♣ Q 5 4
♠ Q 9                          ♠ J 6
♡ J 9 6 4          □          ♡ A Q 10 8
◇ 8 7 3                        ◇ 9 5 2
♣ 10 9 7 6                     ♣ A K J 3
              ♠ A K 8 4 3
              ♡ 3
              ◇ A J 10 6 4
              ♣ 8 2
```

WEST	NORTH	EAST	SOUTH
Pass	Pass	1 NT	2 ♠
Pass	3 ♠	Pass	4 ♠
All Pass			

Opening lead: ♣6.

3. Dlr: South
Vul: N-S

	♠ A K J 5 3	
	♡ A Q 10	
	◇ 7 6	
	♣ A K 10	
♠ 10 4		♠ 9 6 2
♡ J 6 4 3 2	□	♡ 8 7
◇ A 10 8		◇ J 5 4 3 2
♣ Q 5 3		♣ 8 7 2
	♠ Q 8 7	
	♡ K 9 5	
	◇ K Q 9	
	♣ J 9 6 4	

WEST	NORTH	EAST	SOUTH
			Pass
Pass	1 ♠	Pass	2 NT
Pass	6 NT	All Pass	

Opening lead: ♠10.

4. Dlr: South
Vul: N-S

	♠ 8 7 4	
	♡ A Q 4	
	◇ A J 10 3	
	♣ A 8 3	
♠ K J		♠ 10 3
♡ K J 10 9 7 6	□	♡ 8 5
◇ 2		◇ 9 8 7 6 5 4
♣ K Q J 10		♣ 9 4 2
	♠ A Q 9 6 5 2	
	♡ 3 2	
	◇ K Q	
	♣ 7 6 5	

WEST	NORTH	EAST	SOUTH
			1 ♠
2 ♡	3 NT	Pass	4 ♠
All Pass			

Opening lead: ♣K.

5. Dlr: South   ♠ K Q 10 5
     Vul: None   ♡ Q 9 6 3
                 ◇ J 9 3
                 ♣ K 7

West		East
♠ 7 6 4		♠ 9 8 2
♡ 8 5 2	□	♡ A K 4
◇ Q 10 6		◇ K 7 5 4
♣ J 9 5 2		♣ 10 8 3

                 ♠ A J 3
                 ♡ J 10 7
                 ◇ A 8 2
                 ♣ A Q 6 4

WEST	NORTH	EAST	SOUTH
			1 NT
Pass	2 ♣	Pass	2 ◇
Pass	3 NT	All Pass	

Opening lead: ♣2.

6. Dlr: West   ♠ 7 4
     Vul: Both   ♡ 4 2
                 ◇ Q 8
                 ♣ K 10 9 8 6 4 2

West		East
♠ Q J 10 3		♠ 2
♡ Q 10 9 5	□	♡ A 8 7 6 3
◇ 10 7		◇ A 5 3 2
♣ Q J 5		♣ A 7 3

                 ♠ A K 9 8 6 5
                 ♡ K J
                 ◇ K J 9 6 4
                 ♣ –

WEST	NORTH	EAST	SOUTH
Pass	Pass	1♡	Dbl (!)
2♡	Pass	Pass	3♠
Pass	4♣	Pass	4◇
Pass	4♠	Pass	Pass
Dbl	All Pass		

Opening lead: ♡5.

The contract was set *two* tricks. How?

Solutions

1. West, with 13 HCP, knew his partner would play no part in the defence, so he led the ♡7. Declarer won and knocked out the ♣A. West continued with the ♡2, masquerading as a man with a five-card heart suit and no further entry. Now declarer thought he couldn't afford to set up the ninth trick in diamonds, lest the defenders get three hearts and two aces, so he tried for his contract by cashing the three top spades. As it was, this established the *setting* trick – for West!

If West had led a normal fourth-best heart, declarer would have made the contract, judging it safe to dislodge the ◇A.

2. Declarer ruffed the third club, went to dummy with a diamond, and led the ♠10, playing East for Q-9-6 or J-9-6 and trying to induce an error. But when East covered with the jack and declarer won the king, West realized that the Q-9 were equals, and he smoothly dropped the *queen*. Of course, declarer went back to dummy and finessed the ♠8.

Declarer might have gone wrong even if West had played the nine, but the play of the queen was virtually sure to work.

3. Declarer won the opening lead in dummy and played a diamond to the king. West, knowing from the bidding that declarer must have the queen, too, was ready for this – he ducked with the proper degree of indifference. Declarer could have taken the club finesse now and won all thirteen tricks, but he had no reason to believe the ♣Q was right and the ◇A was wrong. He returned to dummy, led another diamond, and went down three!

4. Declarer won the opening lead and tried for quick discards on diamonds. West ruffed the second diamond with the ♠K, cashed two clubs, and exited with the ♡J, won by dummy's queen. Declarer naturally placed East with the rest of the trumps, so he led the ♠8 and passed it. Unlucky!

Had West ruffed with the ♠J, declarer probably would have picked off the now-bare king, playing the opponent who had bid for that card.

5. The opening lead marks declarer with four clubs. The defence has a chance only if declarer has three diamonds and West holds the ◇Q. Even so, it won't help if East shifts to a low diamond. Declarer ducks this to the queen and can always guess right if West continues the suit.

Instead, East should try leading the ◇K (the less pause for thought, the better). Now declarer will fear that East holds K-Q-10-x and West has the remaining high heart for an entry. If declarer ducks, and ducks again when East continues with a low diamond, he is beaten.

6. The famous deal is from the 1963 Bermuda Bowl. Benito Garozzo was East. Winning the ♡A, Garozzo switched to a trump, won by declarer. South now led a diamond to the queen, and Garozzo ducked smoothly! He ducked again when the ◇8 was continued. Reasonably enough, declarer judged to pass the eight, hoping it would drive out the ace from West, and Garozzo had created a second diamond trick from thin air.

Quiz 24

Don't Be End-played!

The side that plays last to a trick enjoys an obvious advantage. In particular, if one side has to break open a brand-new suit, it'll wind up costing them a trick a substantial part of the time. Therefore, a useful technique in play is to exit purposely, forcing the opponents to help you by leading.

Declarers use this technique so often that the defence constantly must be alert. There may be signs that declarer is planning a throw-in (also called an end-play, an elimination or a strip), and there also are ways the defenders may be able to thwart declarer's plans.

```
Dlr: West            ♠ A 4
Vul: Both            ♡ 10 7 4 2
                     ◇ 6 5
                     ♣ Q J 7 5 2
    ♠ 8 2                              ♠ 6 3
    ♡ A K J 3                          ♡ 8 6 5
    ◇ K Q 10 3        □               ◇ J 8 7 4 2
    ♣ K 6 3                            ♣ 10 9 4
                     ♠ K Q J 10 9 7 5
                     ♡ Q 9
                     ◇ A 9
                     ♣ A 8
```

WEST	NORTH	EAST	SOUTH
1 NT	Pass	Pass	4 ♠
All Pass			

South's blast into game was indelicate – a slower approach might have reached the laydown 3 NT. Against the ♠4 contract, West cashed two top hearts and switched to the ◇K. Declarer won and ran off seven rounds of trumps. East threw one card in each red suit and all three clubs, while West came down to the guarded ♣K and the ◇Q. Declarer then led his diamond, end-playing West.

West knew from the discards that declarer had the ace and a small club, so he should have tried to avoid the throw-in by discarding his high diamond, hoping East had the jack.

On many hands, a defender will lack the luxury of picking his discards in comfort. This deal is from the 1980 World Team Olympiad final.

Dlr: East
Vul: None

		♠ J	
		♡ K J 10 8 2	
		◇ K 6 5	
		♣ J 8 4 3	

♠ Q 9 8 5 4		♠ 10 7 6 3
♡ A 7	□	♡ 6 5
◇ A 10 7 4		◇ Q 8 2
♣ Q 6		♣ A 10 7 2

		♠ A K 2	
		♡ Q 9 4 3	
		◇ J 9 3	
		♣ K 9 5	

WEST	NORTH	EAST	SOUTH
		Pass	1 ♣
1 ♠	Dbl	3 ♠	Pass
Pass	Dbl	Pass	4 ♡
All Pass			

Mike Passell, West for the United States, led a spade, won by dummy's jack. Declarer, Henri Szvarc of France, led trumps. Passell took his ace and got out with a trump. Declarer won in hand and led a low diamond. Passell saw the danger and dashed up with the ace, exiting with a diamond to dummy's king. Now declarer came to hand with a trump, cashed his spades, ruffed his last diamond, and led a club to the king. If West had played low here, another club lead would have entangled the defenders in an end-play. But Passell unblocked his queen, and there was nothing declarer could do but lose two more tricks. The United States won ten IMPs when their South, Bobby Wolff, made the same contract at the other table.

That was a solo performance by Passell, but avoiding

end-plays are more often a matter of partnership co-operation.
Edgar Kaplan and Norman Kay collaborated beautifully on this
hand from the 1966 Reisinger Teams.

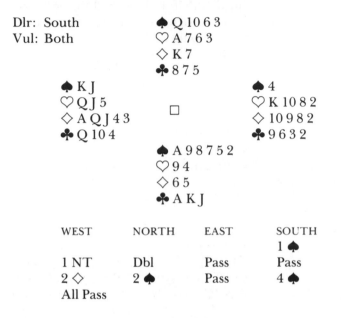

Dlr: South   ♠ Q 10 6 3
Vul: Both   ♡ A 7 6 3
                    ◇ K 7
                    ♣ 8 7 5

♠ K J   ♠ 4
♡ Q J 5   □   ♡ K 10 8 2
◇ A Q J 4 3   ◇ 10 9 8 2
♣ Q 10 4   ♣ 9 6 3 2

                    ♠ A 9 8 7 5 2
                    ♡ 9 4
                    ◇ 6 5
                    ♣ A K J

WEST	NORTH	EAST	SOUTH
			1 ♠
1 NT	Dbl	Pass	Pass
2 ◇	2 ♠	Pass	4 ♠
All Pass			

Kaplan, West, led the ♡Q. Declarer ducked this, and Kay seized
the chance to overtake with the king. Declarer won the club
switch and immediately led a diamond to the jack and king. Kay
subsequently found himself on lead with the ◇10, and another
club lead saved Kaplan from the impending club end-play. The
defence ended with one trick in each suit.

Incidentally, Kaplan knew it was safe to duck the first
diamond lead – declarer could not hold a singleton. Kay almost
certainly had only one spade, and with a five-card diamond suit,
he would have removed 1 NT doubled to 2◇.

Avoiding end-plays requires lots of foresight. On this deal
from a matchpoint event, West had to be careful about his
choice of leads.

Dlr: South
Vul: N-S
Matchpoints

	♠ 6 5 4	
	♡ 9 8 2	
	◇ A K 10 3	
	♣ K J 2	
♠ Q 9 7 3 2		♠ J 8
♡ K J 7 6	□	♡ Q 5 4 3
◇ 7 6		◇ 9 5 2
♣ Q 3		♣ 8 7 6 5
	♠ A K 10	
	♡ A 10	
	◇ Q J 8 4	
	♣ A 10 9 4	

WEST	NORTH	EAST	SOUTH
			1 NT
Pass	3 NT	All Pass	

West led the ♣3 to the jack and king. Declarer cashed four
diamonds, as West discarded two spades, and then misguessed
in clubs, losing a finesse to West's queen. West could count
declarer for 3-2-4-4 pattern, and he felt obliged to switch to
hearts – declarer, who had shown 14 HCP, might well have just
Q-x of hearts. So a low heart lead went to queen and ace.
Declarer then cashed two more clubs, forcing West down to the
♡K and the Q-9 of spades. A heart exit end-played West for a
valuable second overtrick.

West could have saved himself by leading the ♡K, a no-cost
play.

We've seen that the defenders routinely duck winners to
preserve their communication or deceive declarer. However, the
technique may leave declarer holding an exit card for a
throw-in. This deal, which was reported in *The Bridge World*, is
from the 1967 European Championship.

Dlr: South   ♠ A J 7 6 4
Vul: None   ♡ K 10
                  ◇ A 3
                  ♣ A K J 3

♠ Q 9 8 5   ♠ 10 3 2
♡ 9 8 6   ♡ A Q 5 4 2
◇ J 9 4   □   ◇ K 7 5
♣ 8 4 2   ♣ 9 6

                  ♠ K
                  ♡ J 7 3
                  ◇ Q 10 8 6 2
                  ♣ Q 10 7 5

The bidding was not given, but South played in 3 NT. West found the ♡9 lead, and East must have been tempted for a moment to allow dummy's ten to hold. Fortunately, realizing that his partner couldn't have a quick entry, he played off the queen, ace, and a low heart instead. This defence held South to his eight top tricks.

Had East ducked the first heart, declarer could have made the contract by cashing the ♠K, four clubs, and (if East had discarded a spade) the ♠A. Then a heart exit would force East to lead away from the ◇K.

Problems

1.   Dlr: North   ♠ A K J 7
     Vul: None   ♡ 6
                       ◇ A K 4 3 2
                       ♣ 10 7 4

     ♠ 8 6
     ♡ Q J 10 7 3
     ◇ Q 6   □
     ♣ K J 8 6

WEST	NORTH	EAST	SOUTH
	1 ◇	1 ♡	1 ♠[1]
4 ♡	4 ♠	All Pass	

[1] suggests five or more spades

You, West, lead the ♡Q. Partner overtakes with the king and

switches to the ♣2. Declarer plays the three, and your jack wins. How do you continue?

2. Dlr: South   ♠ A 8
    Vul: None   ♡ A K Q J
                         ◇ Q 2
                         ♣ K Q 5 4 3

    ♠ Q J 10 7 2
    ♡ 4 3   □
    ◇ A J 10 9 8 6
    ♣ –

WEST	NORTH	EAST	SOUTH
			Pass
1 ♠	Dbl	Pass	1 NT
2 ◇	3 ◇	Pass	3 NT
All Pass			

The occasion is the 1967 Bermuda Bowl. You are playing for Italy, and as the auction indicates, you like to bid. Against 3 NT you lead the ◇J. Dummy's queen wins, partner playing the seven. At trick two declarer plays a club to his jack. Plan your defence.

Solutions

1. Your play can matter only if declarer has three clubs to the ace and three small diamonds. Think it over before returning the ♣6. If partner has to put up the queen, that will leave you holding your side's club winner. You'll be vulnerable to an end-play.

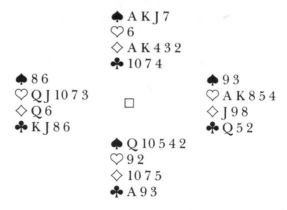

♠ A K J 7
♡ 6
◇ A K 4 3 2
♣ 10 7 4

♠ 8 6
♡ Q J 10 7 3
◇ Q 6
♣ K J 8 6

♠ 9 3
♡ A K 8 5 4
◇ J 9 8
♣ Q 5 2

♠ Q 10 5 4 2
♡ 9 2
◇ 10 7 5
♣ A 9 3

On a low-club return, declarer wins the ace, draws trumps, ruffs the losing heart, cashes the top diamonds, and exits with a club to you. You must give a ruff-and-discard, and declarer's diamond loser disappears. To avoid this ignominy, lead the ♣K at trick three.

Partner did well not to try a deceptive lead of the ♣Q, which would have led to a certain end-play.

2.   Partner appears to have ducked the ♣A! If he has another diamond, you will have a few well-chosen words for him after the session. But for now, consider whether the contract can still be beaten.

Declarer must have the ♠K, so he is up to eight tricks and you are threatened with an end-play. The run of the hearts will force you down to seven cards. No matter what you keep, declarer will be able to end-play you into giving him the ◇K – *if he has the ♠9*. The full deal:

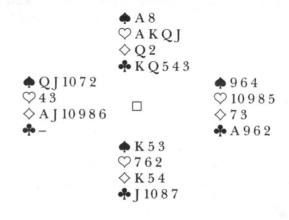

♠ A 8
♡ A K Q J
◇ Q 2
♣ K Q 5 4 3

♠ Q J 10 7 2
♡ 4 3
◇ A J 10 9 8 6
♣ –

♠ 9 6 4
♡ 10 9 8 5
◇ 7 3
♣ A 9 6 2

♠ K 5 3
♡ 7 6 2
◇ K 5 4
♣ J 10 8 7

In 1967, Giorgio Belladonna at once began to discard his spades from the top. By the time declarer finished the hearts, Giorgio had only the seven and two left. Now no end-play was possible, and declarer had to concede down one.

Italy won a swing on the deal when their N-S pair reached the same contract at the other table and West led the ♠Q.

Problems

3. Dlr: West   ♠ 9 8 3
    Vul: Both   ♡ Q 10 7 6
                    ◇ K Q 9
                    ♣ A Q 2

♠ A 7 2
♡ K 5 3
◇ A 10 4   □
♣ K J 10 5

WEST	NORTH	EAST	SOUTH
1 ♣	Pass	Pass	1 ♡
Pass	3 ♡	Pass	4 ♡
All Pass			

You, West, lead the ♣J – queen, nine, three. Declarer plays a heart to the ace and another heart. You win, as East throws the ♠4, and you continue with the ♣K. Declarer wins, draws your last trump (East discarding a low diamond), and leads the ◇K. You win and try the ♣10, but declarer ruffs. He cashes the ◇J and ◇Q, East following. Then comes the ♠9 – ten, queen. How do you defend?

4. Dlr: North   ♠ K 10 5 3
    Vul: None   ♡ J 8 6 3
                    ◇ A K 5
                    ♣ 10 3

                          ♠ 9 8 2
                          ♡ A Q 10 9
                □   ◇ 7
                          ♣ K Q 6 5 4

WEST	NORTH	EAST	SOUTH
	Pass	1 ♣	Dbl
Pass	2 ♣	Pass	2 ♠
Pass	4 ♠	All Pass	

Now it's the 1970 Bermuda Bowl. You lately became a free agent, so you now are playing for Norway. West, your partner, leads the ♡7. Plan your defence.

Solutions

3. Declarer is known to have 3-5-3-2 shape, and he must have the ♠K as well as the queen for his 4♡ bid. Assuming partner has the jack, the six becomes a crucial card. To make sure of beating the contract, you must let the ♠Q hold. The full deal:

```
                    ♠ 9 8 3
                    ♡ Q 10 7 6
                    ◇ K Q 9
                    ♣ A Q 2
   ♠ A 7 2              □          ♠ J 10 5 4
   ♡ K 5 3                         ♡ 4
   ◇ A 10 4              □         ◇ 8 7 6 2
   ♣ K J 10 5                      ♣ 9 8 7 4
                    ♠ K Q 6
                    ♡ A J 9 8 2
                    ◇ J 5 3
                    ♣ 6 3
```

If you win, you must return a spade. Declarer then will make the contract by playing low from dummy – he knows East has the ♠J, since that card would have given you enough to open 1 NT.

4. Partner's lead is a heavy favourite to be a singleton. To avoid later complications, win the ♡A and return the *queen*.

♠ K 10 5 3
♡ J 8 6 3
◇ A K 5
♣ 10 3

♠ 7 6   ♠ 9 8 2
♡ 7   ♡ A Q 10 9
◇ Q 9 6 4 3 2   □   ◇ 7
♣ J 9 7 2   ♣ K Q 6 5 4

♠ A Q J 4
♡ K 5 4 2
◇ J 10 8
♣ A 8

In 1970, East for Norway won the ♡A and returned the nine. Declarer, Bobby Wolff, ducked, and West ruffed. Wolff won the club switch, drew trumps, and finessed in diamonds. After eliminating that suit, he exited with a club. Whichever defender won was end-played. Note that the return of the ♡Q, letting West ruff out the king, would have left declarer with no chance.

In the other room, the contract was 4♡, down, so the United States gained a big swing.

At Your Club: Defence at Duplicate Bridge

At matchpoint duplicate (tournament) bridge, your scores are compared with those of other pairs who hold your cards on an identical deal. The distribution of the cards, the dealer, and the vulnerability are the same every time the deal is played – only the players change. Your *matchpoint* score, which determines whether you win the event, is based on how many of your competitors you beat (by any margin). Very small differences in the scores can swing a lot of matchpoints, and this can profoundly affect your strategy.

```
Dlr: South          ♠ 10 7 4
Vul: N-S            ♡ J 5
Matchpoints        ◇ 6 5 4
                   ♣ A Q J 9 4
                                ♠ 8 6 5 3
                                ♡ A 7
                   □           ◇ Q 10 9 2
                                ♣ 7 3 2
```

WEST	NORTH	EAST	SOUTH
			1 ♡
Pass	1 NT	Pass	3 ♡
Pass	4 ♡	All Pass	

West, your partner, leads the ♠K. Declarer wins the ace and plays a trump to the jack and your ace. What do you return?

There would be no choice at rubber bridge or IMPs – you return the ◇10, since partner must hold the ace if you are to have any chance of setting the contract. But at matchpoints, your goal is not to set the contract but to beat the many other pairs who will defend ♡4 with your cards. (On this deal, the

224

contract is 'normal' – 4♡ will be reached at almost every table –
so the matchpoints will be won in the *play*. This won't always be
the case.)

On the bidding, the ◇A probably resides in declarer's hand,
so at matchpoints you should return a spade and cash what
tricks you can – at least one spade should cash since West might
have bid at the vulnerability with K-Q-J-x-x. If you return a
diamond and find declarer with a hand like

> ♠ A x
> ♡ K Q 10 9 x x
> ◇ A x
> ♣ K x x

your matchpoint score will be poor.

Dlr: South   ♠ 8 6 3
Vul: Both   ♡ K 6 3
Matchpoints   ◇ A 10 9 5 4
             ♣ 8 7

>   ♠ K 10 4
>   ♡ J 10 9 8
> □   ◇ K Q 2
>   ♣ 9 6 3

South opens 1NT (16-18 HCP), and all pass. West, your
partner, leads the ♠5 – three, king, ace. Declarer runs the ◇8 to
your queen, and you return a spade to declarer's queen, West
playing the two. Now the ◇J is passed to your king.

At any other form of scoring, you would return a club, since
partner must have something in clubs to beat the contract. At
matchpoints, though there is a fair case for a spade return,
allowing partner to take his tricks. Declarer will make no more
than two this way, whereas he might make three if you return a
club. (He could have the ♡A and ♣AK, or the ♣A or ♣AJ and
♡AQ.

This hand appeared in a best-selling bridge book, and a spade
return was suggested. In fact, a spade return gains in three
situations, while a club also gains in three: when declarer has the
♣K, ♣KJ, or the ♡Q and ♣AQJ.

Even a *heart* return could be best. If declarer's holding is ♡A
and ♣AQ, he might judge from your failure to return a club

that you have the ♣K and take the club finesse. At any rate, you can see how the matchpoint conditions can give extra headaches to both sides.

Opening leads at matchpoints also demand a different approach. There is a stronger tendency toward safety. Aggressive leads that offer only nebulous hope of beating the contract have less to gain and more to lose at matchpoints. Once again, beating the contract may be a secondary consideration.

WEST	NORTH	EAST	SOUTH
		1 NT	Pass
3 NT	All Pass		

As South you hold

> ♠ K Q 10
> ♡ A 7 5 4 2
> ◇ K 3 2
> ♣ 8 7

Lead the ♠K, making sure of a couple of tricks. The chance of establishing hearts is too uncertain to lead that suit.

WEST	NORTH	EAST	SOUTH
		1 ♠	Pass
2 ♠	Pass	3 ♡	Pass
4 ♡	All Pass		

As South you hold

> ♠ 5
> ♡ K 6 3
> ◇ K Q 10 4
> ♣ K 10 7 5 2

Try the ◇K. Leading the singleton spade would gain a bushel of points when it works, but that's irrelevant at pairs. What matters is that it rates to lose *a trick* more often than it gains one.

WEST	NORTH	EAST	SOUTH
		1 ♡	Pass
3 ♣	Pass	3 ♡	Pass
4 ♣	Pass	4 NT	Pass
5 ♡	Pass	6 NT	All Pass

As South you hold

> ♠ A 10 6 4
> ♡ 9 7 3
> ◇ Q J 10
> ♣ 8 7 3

Cash the ♠ A – there is a good chance the opponents have thirteen tricks as soon as they gain the lead. You might score a lot of matchpoints by holding them to six. You would lead the ◇ Q against an auction like 1 NT-4 NT-6 NT, and even on this auction you might lead a diamond at IMPs or rubber bridge.

At rubber bridge, your goal is scoring as many points as possible. At pairs, some scores are as much as you want or need. You must evaluate the contract and decide what your target should be.

Dlr: West   ♠ 7 6
Vul: N-S   ♡ K Q 7 6
Matchpoints   ◇ A 9 6 2
               ♣ K 8 7

♠ A J 9 5 4		♠ Q 10 8 3 2
♡ 2	□	♡ A 8 5 4 3
◇ K J 8 3		◇ 10 7 5
♣ A 3 2		♣ –

               ♠ K
               ♡ J 10 9
               ◇ Q 4
               ♣ Q J 10 9 6 5 4

WEST	NORTH	EAST	SOUTH
1 ♠	Dbl	4 ♠	5 ♣
Dbl	All Pass		

Thinking E-W are trying to steal, South unsoundly tries 5♣. West leads to the ♡A and receives a ruff. At rubber bridge, he might underlead the ♠A now, hoping for another ruff and a tasty +800. At pairs it is right to *cash* the ♠A. Few Souths will bid 5♣ vulnerable against not, and +500 will beat all the E-W pairs who score +480 in 4♠.

```
Dlr: East           ♠ J 8 4 2
Vul: Both           ♡ J 9 4 2
Matchpoints         ◇ A K 4
                    ♣ 9 8
   ♠ K 7                          ♠ 9 5
   ♡ Q 10 8                       ♡ A 5 3
   ◇ Q 10 9 8 3        □          ◇ J 6 5 2
   ♣ A J 3                        ♣ K 5 4 2
                    ♠ A Q 10 6 3
                    ♡ K 7 6
                    ◇ 7
                    ♣ Q 10 7 6
```

WEST	NORTH	EAST	SOUTH
		Pass	Pass
1 ◇	Pass	1 NT	All Pass

South leads the ♠6. Dummy's king wins, North signalling with the eight. A diamond goes to North's king, and the ♠J is played.

South's decision never to bid looks very doubtful. Declarer probably has the ♡A and ♣K; nevertheless, N-S can make 3♠, and many N-S pairs will get into the bidding one way or another.

South can beat 1 NT one trick by leaving partner on lead to switch to a heart, and that would be the right defence at IMPs. But +100 will be worth few matchpoints if everybody else is +140. Instead, South must go all out for down two (at the risk of letting the contract make) by overtaking the spade and switching to a low heart.

Declarer probably will try dummy's ten, winning the ace when North's jack covers. But when North wins the ◇A, he can lead another spade, and now another low heart from South makes declarer guess.

Problems

1. Dlr: South   ♠ K Q 4 2
     Vul: Both   ♡ A 9 6
                     ◇ K 6
                     ♣ K 8 6 2

                                    ♠ J 10 6 5
                                    ♡ 7 5 4
                          □   ◇ A 9 4
                                    ♣ A J 4

WEST	NORTH	EAST	SOUTH
			1 ♡
Pass	1 ♠	Pass	2 ♡
Pass	4 ♡	All Pass	

West, your partner, leads the ◇J. Dummy's king covers. How do you defend?

2. Dlr: South   ♠ 8 6 3
     Vul: N-S   ♡ A Q 10 6 4
                     ◇ K 4 3
                     ♣ 5 4

                                    ♠ K 7 2
                                    ♡ K 7 5
                          □   ◇ Q 10 9 7
                                    ♣ J 10 7

WEST	NORTH	EAST	SOUTH
			1 ♣
Pass	1 ♡	Pass	2 NT
Pass	3 NT	All Pass	

West, your partner, leads the ♠Q. Plan your defence.

Solutions

1.   Win the ◇A and cash the ♣A. Declarer is likely to have six heart tricks, three spades, and a diamond. If he has either a third diamond to ruff or the ♣Q, you can never do better than hold the hand to five anyway. The full deal is:

```
                    ♠ K Q 4 2
                    ♡ A 9 6
                    ◇ K 6
                    ♣ K 8 6 2
     ♠ 9 8 7                          ♠ J 10 6 5
     ♡ Q                              ♡ 7 5 4
     ◇ J 10 8 7 2     □              ◇ A 9 4
     ♣ 10 9 7 5                       ♣ A J 4
                    ♠ A 3
                    ♡ K J 10 8 3 2
                    ◇ Q 5 3
                    ♣ Q 3
```

If you exit passively at trick two, declarer will squeeze you in the
black suits to make two overtricks. This will give you a
matchpoint zero.

2.

```
                    ♠ 8 6 3
                    ♡ A Q 10 6 4
                    ◇ K 4 3
                    ♣ 5 4
     ♠ Q J 10 5                       ♠ K 7 2
     ♡ 8 2                            ♡ K 7 5
     ◇ J 8 5          □              ◇ Q 10 9 7
     ♣ 9 8 6 3                        ♣ J 10 7
                    ♠ A 9 4
                    ♡ J 9 3
                    ◇ A 6 2
                    ♣ A K Q 2
```

The battle for a single trick in a normal contract can be crucial at
matchpoints. West should have at least Q-J-9-x of spades, so East
can afford to overtake the first trick, trying to look like a man
with K-x. Declarer might win the second round of spades
anyway, since he stands a good chance for twelve tricks if the
heart finesse works; but there is nothing wrong with giving him
a nudge in the wrong direction.

Along the same lines, a defender might decline to overtake
with K-x if he *wants* declarer to hold up an ace twice.

Problems

3. Dlr: South   ♠ K 7
    Vul. N-S   ♡ A K J
                       ◇ A Q 10 7 2
                       ♣ Q 4 3

                                    ♠ A Q 2
                         □   ♡ Q 10 6
                                    ◇ 9 8 5 4
                                    ♣ K J 5

WEST	NORTH	EAST	SOUTH
			Pass
Pass	1 ◇	Pass	1 NT
Pass	3 NT	All Pass	

West, your partner, leads the ♠4. Dummy's king loses to your ace, declarer playing the six. When you cash the ♠Q, declarer plays the eight and West the three. How do you continue?

4. Dlr: South   ♠ A 3
    Vul: None   ♡ 8 3
                       ◇ A J 10 7 6 2
                       ♣ 7 5 4

                                    ♠ 10 8 4
                         □   ♡ K Q 6
                                    ◇ Q 9 8 4
                                    ♣ K J 9

WEST	NORTH	EAST	SOUTH
			1 NT
Pass	3 NT	All Pass	

West, your partner, leads the ♣2. Your king holds the first trick, and your ♣J wins at trick two. How do you continue?

Solutions

3.

```
                          ♠ K 7
                          ♡ A K J
                          ◇ A Q 10 7 2
                          ♣ Q 4 3
        ♠ J 9 5 4 3                        ♠ A Q 2
        ♡ 9 5 4 3            □              ♡ Q 10 6
        ◇ 6                                 ◇ 9 8 5 4
        ♣ 10 7 6                            ♣ K J 5
                          ♠ 10 8 6
                          ♡ 8 7 2
                          ◇ K J 3
                          ♣ A 9 8 2
```

Partner must have the ♠J – if declarer had J-x-x, he could have made sure of a stopper by playing low from dummy. So you can run off five spade tricks for down one and a probable average result. (The bidding marks declarer with the ♣A and ◇K, so he has eight tricks when he gets in.)

A better score is available if you switch to a diamond at trick three. Declarer, thinking you have only two spades, will be gratified at the unexpected chance to make the contract. When he takes the heart finesse for his ninth trick, you can win and switch back to spades for down two.

For a top, however, switch to the ♣J at trick three. Declarer will never believe that any sane East could hold the ♣K. He will go up with the ace and finesse in hearts – down three!

4.   It is likely that declarer is holding up the ♣A. (There is barely room for partner to hold the ace, but in that event you will have a chance to cash out later.)

Partner seems to have found a good opening lead. His ♣2 shows four cards there; he can have no more than one diamond, and he would have preferred to lead a heart or spade with five cards in either suit. So his pattern is 4-4-1-4. At many tables, West will lead a major suit, which may give declarer an extra spade trick or time to set up hearts.

Since there is nothing to gain by continuing clubs, switch to the ♡K, setting up a fourth defensive trick while you still have a probable diamond entry. The full deal:

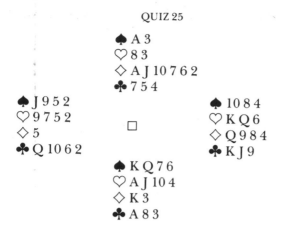

♠ A 3
♡ 8 3
◇ A J 10 7 6 2
♣ 7 5 4

♠ J 9 5 2
♡ 9 7 5 2
◇ 5
♣ Q 10 6 2

□

♠ 10 8 4
♡ K Q 6
◇ Q 9 8 4
♣ K J 9

♠ K Q 7 6
♡ A J 10 4
◇ K 3
♣ A 8 3

At IMPs or rubber bridge, you would try a *low* heart. If declarer
has A-J-9-x and misguesses, you will beat the contract. At pairs,
you do not need to beat the contract to get a good score.
Partner's club lead already has put you ahead of the other pairs,
so do nothing to jeopardize your good score.

Acknowledgements

I certainly make no pretence of having devised every problem in this book independently. I did defend some of the hands; invariably, the ones I remember best are those on which I could have beaten the contract but didn't. I observed several more and constructed still others to illustrate a principle.

However, anyone who compiles a book of this kind is obliged to consult sources. To produce the best possible selections of problems, the author must pore over the works of other bridge writers. He must also search patiently for a theme that the reader will find especially clear and instructive, and that he, the author, can adapt – and perhaps embellish or improve.

Among the writers who provided inspiration in the preparation of this book are:

Albert Dormer; Jeremy Flint; G.C.H. Fox; Charles H. Goren, and others writing under the Goren byline; David Greenwood; Jim Jacoby; Edwin B. Kantar; Edgar Kaplan; H.W. Kelsey; Mike Lawrence; Marshall Miles; Victor Mollo; Terence Reese; Alfred Sheinwold; Alan Truscott; Bobby Wolff and Kit Woolsey

Anyone familiar with bridge literature will recognize that this list contains the names of many of the great journalists of the game, as well as some of its finest players. I wish to recognize their skills and accomplishments, and I am happy to acknowledge my debt to each of them.

Some of the problems originate with deals published in *The Contract Bridge Bulletin* or the annual World Championship book. Both are productions of the hard-working *Bulletin* staff of the American Contract Bridge League, of which I am honoured to be a part. Other problems are based on deals for which my source is *The Bridge World* magazine. *The Bridge World*, which enjoys an international reputation for excellence in the expert community, is an indispensable source for anyone attempting a book of this kind.

My thanks to Edwin B. Kantar and Harold Katz, who graciously checked portions of the original manuscript for analytical error.

For convenience, players are referred to as 'he' throughout this book. This is a conventional device that most bridge books adopt. There are, of course, many fine bridge players of both sexes.